Samaritan Exegesis

A compilation of writings from the Samaritans:

Mount Gerizim: The One True Sanctuary

&

The Book Of Enlightenment: For The Instruction Of The Inquirer

Cover Photography and Textual Revisions, Copyright 2013

by
Nathan Samuel

Cover Photograph of a Samaritan Prayer Book

MOUNT GERIZIM
THE ONE TRUE SANCTUARY

By

COHEN AMRAM ISAAC

**High Priest of the Samaritan Community
Nablus — Israel**

Translated from the Arabic
By
Abdallah ben Kori

Greek Convent Press — Jerusalem

CONCERNING SAMARITAN MANUSCRIPTS

The Samaritan priests, appreciating the interest of American and European Christians, are now willing to sell to them accurate modern copies of the ancient books of the Samaritan religion. I think it well, however, to warn intending purchasers that not all the copies offered for sale, even in Nablus, are accurate. Some people of little learning, relying on the ignorance of the tourists, have made garbled copies of our Torah, and sold them to tourists, or correspondents. Manuscripts purchased at our Synagogue, from myself or my sons will be certified as complete and correct. Several recent purchasers have sent their manuscripts to me for inspection and I have been sorry not to be able to certify to their correctness. It grieves us to have our Law incorrectly copied. I request my friend, Dr. Barton, to make this statement to intending purchasers. We desire that such copies of our sacred books as go forth into Christian libraries shall be accurate. Any manuscript purchased in our Synagogue, and bearing my seal, is genuine and complete.

Priest Amram Isaac,
Samaritan Priest,
President of the Higher Community of the Samaritan Religion
Nablus — Israel

MOUNT GERIZIM - THE ONE TRUE SANCTUARY

AMRAM ISAAC PRESIDENT OF THE HIGHER COMMUNITY OF THE SAMARITAN RELIGION AT SHECHEM

INTRODUCTORY NOTE

The following remarkable paper is by this Priest of the Samaritan religion. It is the living utterance of a sect almost forgotten, and remembered by the world only in connection with its relations, first with the Jews, and afterward with the ministry of Jesus. Through these sources we know that the Samaritans have held throughout the ages a weary and profitless controversy concerning the authorized place of worship. The pilgrim to Jerusalem looses the shoes from off his feet in reverence for that ancient holy place, and casts a curious glance at Gerizim as he rests by Jacob's well, and thinks of it as a shrine established by the excommunicated priest Manasseh and his father-in-law Sanballat in the time of Nehemiah.

Against this judgment on the evidence of one side the High Priest asks to be heard. He claims to be able to show for Gerizim an antiquity far antedating Jerusalem. For the first time in any modern tongue (so far as known to the editor of this document) he has secured the ear of Christendom, and he asks for an impartial hearing.

It will certainly surprise many readers of this article to find the High Priest so keen a logician. While this article shows much reasoning of the type we have learned to call rabbinical, his argument as a whole is logical, and follows the historical method to a climax.

He claims to set forth, as he has received it from his fathers, the Samaritan priests in unbroken succession from Aaron, the argument for the sanctity of the holy mountain, Gerizim, against what he deems the modern and unsupported claims of the Jebusite city called by the Jews Jerusalem. That city, he affirms, was not the place mentioned in the sacred Torah as the one to which the children of Israel were journeying, nor was it known to them, nor was it in their possession, nor is it named in the passages in the Scriptures of the Jews which they quote in support of it. The unnamed sanctuary there cannot refer to Jebus, which was not known to the Jews at that time, nor until David captured it, and his wicked son Solomon introduced idolatry of various kinds. He appeals to the Scriptures of the Jews, and affirms that where the place of the sanctuary is unnamed it cannot refer to Jerusalem, and that where it is named it plainly names Gerizim. There the tribes gathered for the ratifying of the Law, and there they continued to come for the crowning of their kings. Even the son of Solomon came back to Gerizim to be crowned, as the Jews themselves know, and their Scriptures declare. How vain, then, is it for them to assert that their city possesses antiquity and sanctity, when their own writings, even with the corruptions they have made in them, show that Gerizim is the place for worship.

This paper constitutes the second of the ten chapters of the book written by the Priest, referred to in the previous article.

I do not pretend that the publication of the Priest's argument will greatly disturb the conclusions of Christian scholarship. To us it matters little on what mountain men were once taught to worship God; since now the true believer may worship the Father everywhere. But if any importance whatever may be attached to the historical inquiry, the Priest has more to say for his side of the controversy than most modern scholars have suspected.

I acknowledge the ability and courtesy of Professor Abdallah ben Kori whose translation has been a labor of love, and without whose cooperation my own work would have been impossible.

The Editor

THE SANCTITY OF GERIZIM

In the name of the Most Merciful God: This chapter is concerning the belief of the Samaritan people as regards the direction in which they turn themselves in prayer, namely, toward Mount Gerizim. Their authority is manifest from the express commands of the holy Torah. In it we shall prove that this identical mountain is the chosen site, the house of God, Bethel. Upon it the Shekinah was established during the life of our lord Joshua, the son of Nun (upon him be peace and the best of favors); and therefore it should be the place of worship. We shall reply, furthermore, to the Jews, who rejected it, and refute their alleged reasons for substituting another place for it, calling to our proof Scriptures that expressly relate to it.

THE DIVINE REVELALION OF THE TRUE SANCTUARY

The Samaritan people, in the first place; declare that, as a matter of fact and viewed from a rational standpoint the best knowledge is to know the Creator (who is exalted above all); and the best action is to worship him (who is exalted); for by both of these every being is ennobled. And, as the result of the diligent inquiry of thinking people, they have been led to the conviction that the Maker of the world is the Ancient One, whose worship shall be binding, and whose unity should be made evident. The spiritual angels left their abode on high and descended earthward upon that sacred spot wherein appeared his worship (who is exalted), and the belief in His oneness. The spot became, on that account, highly exalted, and quite distinct from every other on the whole earth. This distinction and explanation are satisfactory to thinking minds.

THE SANCTUARY FROM MOSES TO JACOB

The prophets, according to the traditions, from Adam to our lord Moses (on whom be peace), had, doubtless, a direction toward which they turned themselves in their worship of God (who is exalted and honored). Passages may be found in the sacred Book that was brought down upon our lord Moses (on whom be peace) which harmonize with this claim. In fact, God (who is exalted) revealed the region and place through Moses, as will be explained later on, with the help of God (may He be exalted). But among those passages it will be of use to mention the ones in connection with our lord Jacob (on whom be peace).

THE PROMISE IN THE WILDERNESS

Again, we note what our lord Moses (on whom be peace)

mentioned in the song that was sung by himself and his people, the children of Israel, in connection with the incident of the sea, and which is found in Exodus 15:17, meaning as follows: "Thou wilt introduce them, and plant them upon the mountain of thy inheritance, in thy place," down to the passage in the same chapter, whose purport is as follows: "Which thou hast made, O Lord, thy sanctuary. Confirm it, O God, by thy power; thou, O God, who rulest eternally and forever." This prophecy of our lord Moses (on whom be peace) confirms the continuation of the sanctity of that place; for it is connected with the ever existence of God and of His kingdom. Whether by the way of inclusiveness or as a part of the whole, it is God's kingdom; therefore this place is a chosen one.

THERE CAN BE BUT ONE SUCH SANCTUARY

Moreover, what would be of import to our position is the command of God (who is exalted) to destroy the places upon which the foreigners worshiped their gods, namely, upon the high mountains, in the groves, and under every shady tree. He commanded them to demolish their altars, to undermine their enclosures, to burn in fire their temples, to break to pieces their engraved idols, to blot out their names from those places, adding," Do not worship otherwise; but only upon the place which the Lord your God chose from among your tribes that His name may abide therein, and He (Who is exalted) may dwell upon it." The name is plainly indicated in Deuteronomy 12:26, "But thy offerings and thy vows, which thou vowest and consecratest to God, carry and bring over to the place which God chose." This place has been already shown, in another chapter, to exist in the land of Canaan, and we shall refer to it later on.

JERUSALEM CANNOT BE THE SANCTUARY

God preferred this tribe known as the Samaritans to those of the Jews, because of God's approval of the Samaritans over the Jews in reference to the point to which direction in prayer is made. In the manuscript of the Torah which is in the hands of the

Samaritans, the reference concerning the point of direction in prayer is indicated in the past tense, namely, "in the place which He chose." The Jews, however, have in all their manuscripts: "in the place which He hath chosen." The Jews claimed the verb to be future, and that the command was fulfilled under Solomon, the son of David, after the passing of two hundred and thirty years of the possession of the land of Canaan by the children of Israel. Then the Jews began to build the city they call Jerusalem, which, in fact, was built by and captured from the Jebusites under the reign of Solomon's father, David, as we have indicated in the first chapter of this book. But what would render this supposition null and void is the making on the part of God (Who is exalted) an obligatory duty upon His people of Israel, during the days of our lord Moses (upon whom be peace) to bring forth a tenth of the fruit of the land and of its crops, and to set apart whatever is vowed of sheep, oxen, and their first born yearly, and to bring the same before the presence of God to the chosen place, prohibiting their use for sacrifice in the villages and cities. Now it would be wrong to make the tithes binding every year, and to have them used in a special place, while the place is either non-existent or unknown, with no means of finding it out. This certainly cannot be accepted by sane minds; for, necessarily, the place must have been already existent and its whereabouts must have been known before Jerusalem was in the hands of the Jews. What might be an additional proof of the wrong supposition of our opponents, as they claimed, is what God (may He be exalted) made binding in reference to oxen and sheep that are set apart; that is, he prohibited the freedom of using them and of having them kept in the hands of him who would set them apart. He, indeed, specified the period to which their setting apart must take place, which is, in case of the oxen, according as it is recorded, up to the time when the oxen reach the age of usefulness, say, in ploughing the earth, and, then, they cannot remain in the hands of their consecrators; for said God (who is exalted): "Do not plough with the first-born of thy ox." This means that the ox ought to be brought to the house of God (who is exalted) before it reaches its age of usefulness. The period limiting the consecration of the first-born of sheep is before the sheep reach what God (who is exalted) specified in the following: "Do not shear the first-born of thy sheep: but before the Lord thy God thou shalt offer it yearly, in the place the Lord thy God chose for thee."

These arguments prove that there was a place of worship known to the fathers and to which they took their sacrifices; and that before Jerusalem was known. We will now consider the reasons why this people claim that direction in prayer is towards, and the worship of God (Who is exalted) is upon, the mountain, which is the mountain of worship for those who devoted themselves to God (Who is exalted).

GERIZIM WAS THE HOME OF ABRAHAM

First, what befell our lord Abraham (upon whom be peace) after God (Who is exalted) commanded him to depart from his land and native home, and said to him, "Go to the land which I shall reveal unto thee, and wherein I shall make thee a great people, and bless thee." The Lord (Who is exalted) tells us that Abraham (upon whom be peace) departed, following His command, and came to the land of Canaan, and journeyed in it till he entered Nablus, that is to "the meadow of Moreh," which is known scripturally and traditionally to be identical with Nablus. It is thus definitely located in the book of Genesis (chap. 12), the contents of which affirm that it is the place in view, where our lord Abraham (upon whom be peace) pitched his tent. Here, as he remained for a while and settled down, God (may He be exalted) appeared to him, and conversed with him, and blessed him, and promised to give him, and his seed, that land (see aforementioned chapter). We can easily conjecture from the contents that God commanded our lord Abraham (upon whom be peace) to leave his country only in order that he might bring him to that place, and we are certain that this place was the one he had promised to direct him to. A sure indication was the fact that the altar was built upon it, and the altar denotes the direction in prayer, as well as the place of prayer and blessing; for upon Abraham's arrival God (may He be exalted) blessed him, and made gifts to him, and he, through the prophetic spirit, felt as if his object would be accomplished in doing pilgrimage to that mountain nearby, as it is recorded in the same chapter, where it says, "And he departed from there to the mountain east of Bethel, and pitched there his tent, Bethel on the west and Ai on the east, and he built there an altar to God, and invoked the name of God." It becomes plain, therefore, that the mountain by the side of the meadow of Moreh is between the mountain of Gerizim and of Ebal (Deuteronomy 11:30). These boundaries and other indications make plain to us the location of the plain of Moreh, and also the mountain of Gerizim. Here is the Bethel. Here our lord Abraham (upon whom be peace) established the altar of worship, and thereupon he declared the name of God (may He be exalted), in order to inform us that the mountain is chosen for that end. The fact is well known that "*Elon Moreh*" is the plain of Beha, and Ai is a village east of that plain, and these boundaries are thrice mentioned in the Samaritan Torah, — twice in the Decalogue (once in its first division, and another time in its second division). The Jews, however, dropped it out from the Decalogue. The reason whereof is that the dignity and virtue of Mount Gerizim is well affirmed therein. There remained, nevertheless, in the Jewish scriptures, the boundaries as we have mentioned them in Deuteronomy 11. The Jews struck out the saying of God (Who is exalted), "confronting Nablus (Shechem)": for the Samaritans' says, "By the side of *Elon Moreh*, which is by the side of Nablus (Shechem)." But though they have struck out God's saying "confronting Nablus," the boundaries that are mentioned in their own text are in favor of our argument. The fame of the mountains of Gerizim and of Ebal is, indeed, great, even in the manuscript of the Jews. The boundaries therein recorded define both sides of the plain: Gerizim on its right, Ebal on its left; and the meadow of Moreh is at the base of Gerizim, reaching as far as the base of Ebal, and Gilgal is opposite the two mountains, and forms a part of their boundaries. To this the intelligent will readily assent. If there were no distinct difference between these two mountains, their boundaries would not have been marked in so specific a manner: such a distinction and preference for the mountain of Gerizim as against the mountain of Ebal will be noticed in its own place in this chapter.

And what would assure us that Nablus and its mountain are the place to which God (may He be exalted) directed our lord Abraham (upon whom be peace): "to the land which I shall show thee", is the great distance he had to go. The departure of our lord Abraham (upon whom be peace) was from "the Ur of Kashdim (Chaldeans), which is in the land of Khorasan". None can make little of the distance between Khorasan and Nablus, to which he went. With all that the holy Torah did not mention any stopping-place or the visiting of any place by our lord Abraham (upon whom be peace) while on his distant journey, except his destination, the place of Nablus, the plain and the mountain confronting it: for they were his sought object, and through them was fulfilled what was promised to our lord Abraham (upon whom be peace) of blessings from his Abundance (may He exalted). Thus it is affirmed that Nablus is a chosen place, and its mountain is a chosen place; it is the mountain of blessing, as it is so explained, and told according to the plain statement of our lord Moses (upon whom be peace); for its name is given as Bethel.

GERIZIM IS THE PLACE OF THE SACRIFICE OF ISAAC

The second argument for affirming that it is the chosen place of worship to God from eternity is that the holy men went to it, and worshiped God upon it, and made pilgrimage of it, and recognized it well. Most notable is the account given as to the trial of our lord Abraham (upon whom be peace) when God (may He be exalted) required the sacrifice of Isaac (upon whom be peace), which is plainly given in Genesis 22. Therein it is said; "After these words God tried Abraham and spoke to Abraham, and he answered, 'Behold, here I am.' And God said, Take thy son, thy only son whom thou lovest, Isaac, and go to that land, the Moreh, and offer him as an offering upon one of the mountains which I will tell you."

Our lord Abraham (upon him be peace) obeyed the order given

him and rose up early, and took his son, our lord Isaac (upon him be peace) and took with him wood for the offering, and took a knife with him and also his servants; and moved in the direction of the place as it is indicated in the chapter mentioned. He saw the place to be very distant; and departed in that direction — to the land of Moreh, after he has gone a distance of three days. Now what is meant by the land of Moreh is where he stopped. It is the land of the plain of Moreh by Nablus, and this must have been the place where God (may He be exalted) commanded him to go. Then our lord Abraham (upon him be peace) looked out to that mountain from afar, and knew positively it was the mountain of Gerizim; for on account of its fame and height, one can see it from afar. The distance proves also that: our lord Abraham (upon whom be peace), when the revelation was given him, was living in the Bir of the Sabi (Beer-sheba), and that is the exact distance between that place and Mount Gerizim; for if a man would depart early from the Bir of the Sabi, he would not arrive at that mountain except upon the third day. This is clearly not at all true to the place claimed by the Jews as that of the sacrifice, for it cannot be see even at a distance of half a day, not to mention three days. If due time our lord Abraham (upon whom be peace) arrived at the mountain, of which he was told, and there he built the altar, that is, the altar which he had built before, meaning, he built it again. It is not said, "He built there *an* altar," as if it were the first time he had done so; but "*the* altar"; for where the letters aleph and lamed are prefixed to an indefinite noun, these letters make it definite, and connect the altar thus rebuilt with a previous and known history. There God (may He be exalted) redeemed our lord Isaac (upon whom be peace) by a ram which he sent, and which our lord Abraham (upon whom be peace) offered in lieu of his son. Thus was fulfilled his prayer, namely: "May God attend to the sheep for offering, my son," which was uttered as a reply to the question of his son concerning the sheep of the offering. Thus God answered his prayer, and looked upon him with His mercy, and redeemed his son for him, and saved him from the edge of the knife. Therefore our lord Abraham (upon whom be peace) called the name of that place GOD-IS SEEN." This name was given for two reasons: first, because God (may He be exalted) saw Abraham (upon whom be peace) with His mercy, and answered him; secondly, because it is a derivation of that place whose name is the land of Moreh wherein the mountain was situated. The same expression is given in the Torah when it was brought down upon our lord Moses (upon whom be peace); it is stated: "And Abraham called the name of that place *YHWH-Jireh*," that is, "GOD-IS-SEEN." The report of this expression was given out by the tongue of our lord Moses (upon whom be peace) when he said: "It is said today. In the mountain *YHWH* shall be seen," for the fame of this mountain was well spread among the children of Israel, during the days of the prophet Moses (upon whom be peace), to the effect that it is the place of prayer and the *Kiblah* ("direction") of those who pray.

Those who are friendly descendants of Abraham (upon whom be peace); besides affirming the foregoing basing their stand upon the Infallible revelation, believe the advantages accrued in this mountain exist still for the benefit of the latter generations. This could be used to subvert the Jews claiming that the chosen place was selected by God (may He be exalted) only through David and Solomon adding in their copy of the Torah that it was a place "to be chosen," we have, therefore, thus produced convincing passages out of the Scriptures, and have proved that the *Kiblah* ("direction" of prayer and pilgrimage) was chosen from eternity.

GERIZIM IS THE BETHEL OF JACOB'S VISION

The third argument can be developed out of the life of our lord Jacob (upon whom be peace). Both the Samaritan and the Jewish copies agree on what was reported in Genesis 28 as to his departure to his uncle, and as to what he met in that place where he tarried the night in dreaming that dream and in seeing those visions. From these incidents the high standing of that place, being the gate of heaven, its distinction from other mountains, the necessity of directing oneself toward it in prayer, and its being the *Kiblah* of the saints are strongly confirmed. We have said something along this line in the first part of this chapter.

The fourth argument is, our lord Jacob (upon whom be peace) arrived safely from his journey which was accomplished by God's providence as is indicated in Genesis 31:13 where God says, "I am the God of Bethel, where thou anointedst a pillar and didst vow a vow; arise and go to the land of thy nativity," While on the mountain, as he was on his way, he vowed as follows: "if God will be with me and will keep me in this way which I go, and will give me bread as food and clothes to put on and if I return in peace to the house of my father; God shall be my lord, and this stone that I have set shall be the house of God: and whatever thou shall give me, that I shall surely tithe for thee." When the Lord (may He by exalted) favored him, and gave him blessings and brought him back in peace, and fulfilled his request, and conferred upon him His favors, He imposed it a duty upon him to fulfill his vows. He reminded him of his pillar and promise, and told him to go to that very place wherein he made his vow, there to fulfill Jacob loaded with abundant favors, obediently left his uncle, and came in the direction of Nablus, for it was the intended place (see Genesis 33:18) "And Jacob came safely to Shechem, which is Nablus which is in the land of Canaan, when he came from Paddan-aram and he pitched his tent before the city."

Now, the single return of Jacob to the city of Nablus is the fulfillment of his prayer which he uttered in the course of his vow, saying, "And if I return safely to the house of my father." Verily, it was the fulfillment of what he wished. By "the house of his father" it means the altar his grandfather Abraham (upon whom be peace) has built in the plain at Nablus, and it is the very one previously mentioned as "*Elon Moreh.*" Therefore our lord Jacob (upon whom be peace) pitched his tent in that place. "He pitched his tent before that city." The city is Nablus. He also bought that plain, to which reference has been made, from the people of that day, and which is called "*Halkat us-Shadi.*" The name of the plain was as first "*Elon Moreh,*" but now it is "*Halkat us-Shadi.*" What stronger argument could there be than the fact that our lord Jacob (upon whom be peace) bought this plain to the neglect of others; that he erected therein an altar and called the name of that altar "The Mighty God of Israel"? This parcel of "*us-Shadi*" belonging to Nablus is at the base of Mount Gerizim. Both the Samaritan and Jewish people agree upon its name and fame. At its corner our lord Joseph (upon whom be peace) is buried. His tomb is still to be seen in it until this very day. This fact is strongly affirmed by the written traditions of both of the mentioned people, so we have exact and undisputed knowledge so far as that place is concerned.

The Samaritan people know these truths through what has been written about it in the books of their forefathers and through their dwelling nearby it.

THE BURIAL OF JOSEPH PROVES THE SANCTITY OF GERIZIM

With the Jews, what affirms our position is the thirty-second verse of the twenty-fourth chapter of Joshua reading as follows: "And the bones of Joseph, which the children of Israel brought up out of Egypt, they buried in Shechem, which place was bought for one hundred sheep. And it became a possession of the children of Joseph." But the Samaritan people explain, from the Scriptures and traditions of their forefathers, that the cause of their forefather Jacob's buying this parcel of land was its exalted rank, because our Lord Abraham (upon whom be peace) erected upon it an altar, and because of its nearness to Mount Gerizim. The burial of our lord Joseph (upon whom be peace) is in that very place. This has been our contention throughout the long discussion with the aforesaid people. Apparently, the burial of Joseph (upon whom be peace) was the result of a special revelation from God (may He be exalted) to our lord Joshua (upon whom be peace), for it was among that section of Nablus given to our lord Joseph (upon whom be peace) by his father Jacob (upon whom be peace). This is explained in Genesis 48:21, "And I gave the Nablus (Sam. Heb. reads Shechem) in preference to thy brothers, which I took from the hand of the Amorite with my sword and bow."

This passage, taken from the Hebrew text, harmonizes with the passage found in the Samaritan text, and also with the text used by the Jews. Accordingly the lord Joshua (upon whom be peace) and the people with him, who found favor in God's sight, gave Nablus and its dependencies to the children of Joseph (upon whom be peace), wherein they buried their grandfather.

We do not admit the claim of the Jews, to the effect that Nablus was one of the cities of Refuge, as is found in their book of Joshua. Now, the cities of Refuge belonged to the children of Levi: observe, therefore, this contradiction. Joseph (upon whom be peace) was buried in his own portion, as it is admitted by both Samaritans and Jews and as we explained previously, and not in land belonging to the Levites (upon whom be peace).

The reason why our lord Jacob (upon whom be peace) gave particularly Nablus to our lord Joseph (upon whom be peace) in preference to his brothers can be found in Jacob's desire to recompense his son's beneficent deeds and favor which the latter accorded to his father and brothers in supplying with abundance their deficiencies and needs in those years of famine, as the report is given in Genesis 47:12 where we find the following: "And Joseph nourished his father, brothers, and all his father's family, with bread according to their families."

He used to feed them, and give them bread, to each in sufficient quantity, including even their children. There was no bread in all the land, for famine was felt sorely. Therefore Jacob (upon whom be peace) gave the noblest of the earth's spots especially to him. And God (may He be exalted) made it a duty upon any of the children of Israel who was to take possession of his own inheritance, wherever it might be, to come to this spot, in order to be sanctified by trading on it, and in order to receive a blessing from it, and thence to carry such a blessing to his own land. And notice of this is given in the book of Deuteronomy 33:13, in the blessing recorded by our lord Moses (upon whom be peace) concerning our lord Joseph (upon whom be peace): "And of Joseph he said, Blessed of the Lord be his land for the precious giving of heaven." This is the land which was given to him and wherein he was buried; it is the blessed land from God (may He be exalted). Blessed shall be those who make pilgrimage to it, and those who dwell upon it: this passage confirms the fact that Nablus and its mountain are chosen by God (may He be glorified). He sanctified them, and blessed them, and made them a worthy site for His worship, and for the fulfilling of vows therein.

GERIZIM WAS THE PLACE TO WHICH JACOB WENT UP TO WORSHIP

The fifth argument can be drawn from the following: that the Scripture declares the place called Bethel to be the chosen site and identified with Mount Gerizim is plain from the account of what took place between our lord Jacob (upon whom be peace) and Shekim the son of Hamor, who was the governor of Nablus in those days, in regard to the latter's marriage with Jacob's daughter Dinah. When Jacob's sons killed the inhabitants of Nablus, our lord Jacob (upon who be peace) became afraid of the consequences of their action, and the Creator (may He be exalted) knew of his fear and revealed to him His will as follows: "Arise, and go up to Bethel, and remain there and erect an altar to the Omnipotent, who appeared to thee in thy flight from before thy brother Esau." Our lord Jacob (upon whom be peace) was at that time living in the land-parcel which he bought from the Amorites, which is *Elon Moreh*, which is close by Mount Gerizim, as we have explained previously. Now when God (may He be exalted) said to Jacob (upon whom be peace): "Go up," He meant that he who desires to go up to Mount Gerizim from this land-parcel, his doing so is a continuous going up from the beginning of his march until his arrival. Furthermore it is explained that this place, upon which Jacob (upon whom be peace) was commanded to go, was the very place where he tarried the night in his flight from his brother Esau. It was there that the angel appeared to him. He called that place Bethel, and erected a pillar upon it. In the account (to which reference has been made) Jacob (upon whom be peace) is commanded to erect another altar on it, in order that the timid may be well assured that such a place is his refuge, for it is the house of God, the protector, (may He be exalted) who saves the one taking refuge in Him and seeking Him by faith, in this place. Our lord Jacob (upon whom be peace) obeyed, and performed, as the Holy Spirit told him, what is dutiful to everyone intending to make a pilgrimage to this place. It was what had been performed, also by his forefathers. He ordered his children to put away from among them the foreign gods, which they had stolen from the worship houses of the people of Nablus. He ordered them to purify themselves, and to change their clothes, as is given in Genesis 35:6. Thereupon he commanded them to go up to *Luzah*, to Bethel, as it is said in the same chapter: "So Jacob came to *Luzah*, which is in Canaan, that is Bethel, he and all the people that were with him." These passages indicate that the place is one, and there is no other included. It belongs to God, and, it was not substituted. It was called, formerly, *Luzah*, but now it is called Bethel. How could there be doubt of its being the chosen place, when its former name "*Luzah*" means "to God" and its following name "Bethel" means "the house of the Almighty"? It was, moreover, called "*Beth-Elohim*," meaning "the house of angels," also "*Sheer-hashamain*," meaning "the gates of heavens". The name "*Gerizim*" appeared for the first time only during the life of our lord Moses (upon whom be peace). He who knows Hebrew and has it at his command can hardly fail to see strong proofs and plain indications in these names, as they are pronounced in Hebrew, and it takes little consideration of these legal and Mosaic passages to come to the sure conclusion that they designate Mount Gerizim or Bethel, meaning "the house of God"; that it is the *Kiblah* for the worship of God (Who is exalted) and the proper site for His descending glory: that it is the place designated by the apostle Moses (upon whom be peace) in Exodus 15:17, while he was praying to God that the people of Israel might remain firm in this mountain, as follows: "Thou shalt bring them in, and plant them in the mountain of thine inheritance, in the place, O Lord, which thou has made for thee to dwell in; in the sanctuary, O, Lord, which thy hands have established. Thou, O Lord, shalt reign forever and ever." From these passages it appears that the place in question is holy, and that its holiness is subject to no change with God (Who is exalted).

GERIZIM IS THE MOUNTAIN WHERE JOSHUA SET UP THE PILLAR

The sixth argument we can have from what is related in the book of Joshua, the one which is in the possession of the Samaritans and according to the one in the possession of the Jews, that the aforesaid mountain is sanctified to God. The Jewish book called Joshua, in chapter 24 verse 25-26, says: "And Joshua made a covenant in that day: he set thereon a statute and an ordinance in Nablus, and wrote all these sayings in the law of God, and he took a large stone, and under the *Hailah*, the oak, that was in the sanctuary of God. This "*Hailah*" is the one under which our lord Jacob (upon whom be peace) buried the spoils his children took from Nablus, when he came up to this mountain, as it is seen in Genesis 35:4, "And they gave unto Jacob all the foreign gods which were in their hands, and the rings which were in their ears; and Jacob hid them under the oak which was by Shechem." Thus it is clear from this and other passages that the sanctuary of God was in Nablus, and that it is the place wherein existed "*Hailah*," whose fame is great with the Samaritans until this day. Even the Muslims who live nearby or in Nablus receive blessings from it, and, following the manner of the children of Israel, call it, "The Pillar," deriving this name from the pillar which our lord Joshua (upon whom be peace) set, and whereupon he wrote the covenant which he made with the children of Israel just before his death, as previously mentioned.

THE TENTH COMMANDMENT REQUIRES WORSHIP IN GERIZIM

The seventh argument is that in the Samaritan Torah, in the Decalogue, in the tenth commandment, there is the following: "And it shall be that when God shall bring thee into the land of the Canaanite, which thou shalt enter to inherit it: there shalt thou set up large stones, and thou shalt plaster them with plaster, and thou shalt write upon the stones all the words of this law.

And when ye shall cross the Jordan, ye shall set up these stones, as I am commanding you, in Mount Gerizim. And ye shall build there an altar for the Lord your God, and thou shalt offer thereupon offerings for the Lord your God: and this mountain is beyond Jordan, towards where the sun sets, in the land of the Canaanite, who dwells in the Arabah opposite Gilgal, beside *Elon Moreh*, in front of Nablus."

This commandment of the Decalogue was omitted by the Jews in their copy. If they would investigate, they would find their Decalogue to be formed of nine commandments. But this commandment was repeated again before the death of our lord the Apostle Moses (upon whom be peace). He made a covenant with them and reminded them of this commandment still found in Deuteronomy 17:1 in the copies of both Samaritans and Jews: "And Moses and the elders of Israel commanded the people, saying. Keep all the commandments I commanded you this day. And when ye shall cross the Jordan to the land the Lord God shall grant thee, then set thee up large stones, and plaster them with plaster, and write upon them all the words of the law. When thou shall cross into the land the Lord your God shall give you, a land that produces milk and honey, as said the Lord the God of your fathers when ye shall cross over, ye shall set up these stones which I command you this day."

Now in the Samaritan Torah the stones are ordered to be set up "in Mount Gerizim"; while the Jews have "in Mount Ebal." It continues: "And thou shalt plaster them with plaster, and thou shalt erect an altar to the Lord thy God, an altar of stones; thou shalt not lift upon them any iron. Of whole stones shall thou build the altar of the Lord thy God, and thou shalt offer upon it burnt offerings to the Lord thy God, and thou shalt offer peace sacrifices. Thou shalt eat there and rejoice before the Lord thy God. He repeated the same though again in this chapter, and made it a duty to have the blessing recited from upon Mount Gerizim, because of the descent of the blessing in this mountain upon the children of Israel. Therefore he said: "These should stand upon Mount Gerizim to bless the people." They were

Simon, Levi, Judah, Issachar, Joseph, and Benjamin; opposite them, according to the command of God (who is exalted), stood six others, upon Mount Ebal as it is said; "And these should stand upon Mount Ebal to curse." They were Reuben, Gad, Asher, Zebulun, Dan, and Naphtali. Following these passages, this change made by the Jews becomes plain; they claim the altar was to be built on Mount Ebal, whereas God (who is exalted) made known to us, through the preceding passages, the exalted difference of Mount Gerizim from Mount Ebal. He told us what to do: to rejoice in that place, where he commanded an altar to be erected thereupon to offer sacrifice and to do other specified things: but joy cannot take place in Mount Ebal, on account of what he commanded to be done upon it, namely, to curse and threaten, which, rather, causes repentance and weeping. Sadness would take hold of the feelings, and if those curses and threatenings were heard one would necessarily weep and repent. All this opposes joy. But the blessings and promises are heard together with other concomitant expressions, namely, blessing God's name; then joy would result. Gladness will possess the feelings; for blessings contain promises of the abundance of wealth, descent of blessing, assurance of victory, and fulfillment of covenant. Prayer must be accompanied with His name (who is exalted). Thus he said to the children of Aaron, who were ordered to bless continually the people of God, Israel, as in Numbers 6:22-27, "And God spoke to Aaron and his sons, saying: Thus ye shall bless the children of Israel" as far as "And they shall place my name upon the children of Israel and I shall bless them." It is proved, therefore, that blessing must be joined with God's name; that God (may He be exalted) established a place wherein it is good to hear it; that the latter can be obtained upon Mount Gerizim. Thus it is written in Deuteronomy 11:29, "And thou shalt perform the blessings upon Mount Gerizim and the cursings upon Mount Ebal." Hence to ask for the blessings and to obtain them must occur only upon this mountain upon which God (may he be exalted) made it imperative to have thanksgiving, sacrificial offerings, and rejoicing, associated with hearing the blessings, as they take place upon Mount Gerizim. The Jews, however, still keep with no alteration the two previously recorded commands in regard to Mount Gerizim, namely: "Thou shalt give the blessings upon Mount Gerizim" and also: "Those shall stand on Mount Gerizim to bless the people." But in connection with the altar, sacrificial offerings, and rejoicing, they change Gerizim to Ebal and, thereby, unite two impossibilities, namely, of having cursing and rejoicing take place jointly, as we have already said. But, at any rate, the erection of an altar as well as the offering of sacrifices and rejoicing must take place in a sacred place, well fitted for that end; for such must be done "before God." It must be attended to as soon as possession of the land shall become a fact. God made it imperative that it should take place only in the site chosen as His *Kiblah*, as several passages of the Scriptures testify to it. He connected the offering of sacrifices with the Tabernacle: whosoever offered sacrifices outside of the tabernacle was caused to perish. He (Who is exalted) commanded that the tabernacle should be erected in the appointed place; He made both the tabernacle and the place eternally indissoluble the one from the other.

As for the conditions of sacrificial offerings before the presence of God, that is, in the *Kiblah* of God, they are found in Leviticus, in several chapters, among which is the seventeenth. Let the reader look this up, and its contents will be found clear. As to the indissoluble connection of the tabernacle with its appointed site, we find several chapters that refer to it, among which is Deuteronomy 12. In this chapter God (may He be exalted) set and designated the appointed place; what must be done upon it; the sacrificial offerings and the rejoicing. From it, it is clear that rejoicing should be done in the tabernacle in the appointed place, and that assures us that the appointed place is Mount Gerizim, which is by Nablus. As to whether it is Mount Gerizim (according to the Samaritans) or Ebal (according to the Jews) in connection with the erection of an altar, the offerings and rejoicing, taking place "before God," that question has been answered. The Law must be read after the passing of the "seven years" The reading must be done in the hearing of all the children of Israel (see Deuteronomy 31:9-12). Also the passover offering must be done in connection with "the appointed place," and not in the temple house, as the Jews claim, and in no other place. The necessary pilgrimages are three every year. Such pilgrimages, according to God's command, must be rendered in His presence, in His appointed place. It is found in Joshua that our lord Joshua (upon whom be peace) left undone not even a word of the Law, but he executed it. The land rested in his days (see Joshua 11:15; 8:35). At the close of the latter chapter we read, "He did not neglect even one word of what Moses commanded; he executed everything."

GERIZIM IS THE MOUNT OF BLESSING

The eighth argument, which also confirms the fact that Mount Gerizim is the appointed place, is that it was the mountain upon which the blessings were recited. Now I will draw the contrast between the exalted estate of Mount Gerizim and that of Mount Ebal, in addition to what preceded.

1. We note the appointment of the first six tribes to stand on Mount Gerizim for blessing; while the other six tribes, all lower in nobility, were designated to stand on Mount Ebal. The tribes upon Ebal were, with the exception of two, the children of concubines. As to Reuben and Zebulun, there is discussion that, for time and space, we shall let go by in this short essay.

2. The necessity of giving the blessings on Mount Gerizim and the cursings on Mount Ebal.

3. When the two mountains are named, Gerizim is always mentioned first.

4. The very appearance of the two mountains suggests a contrast, and discloses the existence of traces of blessings on Mount Gerizim. It is a shining mountain. It is crowned with water springs gushing from all its sides. It has full vegetation and a healthy climate. Mount Ebal has nothing of the kind as we can see today.

5. The fact that it is called "*Bethel*," and that "*Elon Moreh*" is by its side. The latter is also called "*Halkat us-Shadi*." No explanation is needed here for the one who looks upon and reads the books of Moses (upon whom be peace). From every standpoint Mount Gerizim towers over Ebal, and is in every possible way superior to it in all points of excellency.

6. There is in the Samaritan Torah the passage that the erection of the altar and the offering of sacrifices should take place on Gerizim. This is the true reading. Contrary to what the Jews affirm, corrupting the very Torah to prove their position, changing the one true place of worship, first to Shiloh and afterward to Jebus, and causing their Law to read that the holy altar was erected on Ebal the mountain of cursing, the Samaritans preserve and obey the word as it was revealed through Moses (upon whom be peace).

7. The Jews forgot Nablus and its exalted state, in spite of the fact that in the days of Samuel and Saul, as it is evident from their own books of Kings and Chronicles, they never used to declare allegiance to a monarch or crown a king except in Shechem (Nablus): for it was the capital of the Kingdom of Israel, and in the lot of our lord Joseph (upon whom be peace), who is the first king that appeared out of the descendants of our lord Jacob (upon whom be peace). (See Kings 12:1 for the coronation of Rehoboam.)

THE TWICE SEVEN HOLY NAMES OF MOUNT GERIZIM

The Samaritan books have for Mount Gerizim twice seven, holy names.

1. The first name is "THE ANCIENT MOUNTAIN." The Ancient One (may He be exalted) chose it from the creation, from the time he made the dry land to appear. It is so designated in Deuteronomy 33:15, wherein the blessing of Joseph (upon whom be peace) it is stated that his blessing shall be from the excellencies of "the ancient mountain."

2. It is called *BETH-EL* meaning "THE HOUSE OF THE ALMIGHTY." The Almighty (may He be exalted) caused it to be a shield and a help to the one making pilgrimage to it. He made it a refuge and sanctuary to all those who turn to God (may He be exalted) and seek Him upon it. This name was mentioned several times in Jacob's flight for his fear of those of Nablus, that is, those who live in or by it. God (may he be exalted) told him. "Arise, and go up to Bethel." A full discussion of the same has already been made in this chapter, and God (may He be exalted) knows best.

3. The third name is "THE HOUSE OF ANGELS" (*Elohim*). It is the dwelling of the holy angels. They never abandon it; they continually remain in it, praising God (may He be exalted) and praying to him on it. Our lord Jacob (upon whom be peace) uttered this name when he said: "This is no other than the house of *Elohim*" (Genesis 28:17).

4. The fourth name is "THE GATE OF HEAVEN." Everyone who prays and seeks God (may He be exalted) in prayer, must direct himself to it. To prove it, see what our lord Jacob (upon whom be peace) said in the same chapter, namely. "And this is the gate of heaven."

5. The fifth name is *LUZAH*. It is declared in the same chapter that the name of the city was at first, *Luzah*. That was its surname from the beginning; for in the first ages they used to designate this mountain, saying. "To him is this *Lozeh*, that is, "TO GOD IS THIS PLACE." This was because of what they used to see of its greatness and lights and this was the reason why our lord Jacob (upon whom be peace) said about this mountain: "How full of lights is this place" (see preceding chapter).

6. The sixth name is "SANCTUARY." It is spoken of as the dwelling of the Holy One (may He be exalted), and it is the place of the sanctuary and the *Kiblah* of the sanctiful people. All these words fit it closely. It is the place of God (may He be exalted): therefore spoke the great prophet Moses (upon whom be peace) in this

holy Torah, as designated in this mountain: "Thou hast made a *sanctuary*, O Lord."

7. The seventh name is "MOUNT GERIZIM." It is explained after the scriptures as the mountain of blessing: "Thou shalt make *the blessing upon Mount Gerizim.*" It is also, hinted at as the dwelling of God (may He be exalted) whereupon the name of God (may He be exalted) must be uttered. Compare: "In the place where my name is pronounced, there I shall be, and I shall bless thee."

8. The eighth name is "*BETH-YHWH.*" This is the very name of the Highest. Compare Exodus 23:19, "The firstlings of thy land shalt thou bring to the house of the Lord (*Beth-YHWH*) thy God." It is the place of offerings of tithes, firstlings, sacrifices and presents, and of everything that belongs to God (may He be exalted), according to his Command. And as there is no companion to the Owner of the name *YHWH*, so there is among all the mountains none like this mountain.

9. The ninth name is "THE BEAUTIFUL MOUNTAIN." Compare Deuteronomy 3:25, where our lord Moses (upon whom be peace) designated so in his prayer that he may enter the holy land in order to see the beautiful mountain: "Let me go beyond to the good land, which is across the Jordan, that beautiful mountain and Lebanon." He meant by that "beautiful mountain" Mount Gerizim; he was praying in its direction as he called it so. The reason of thus surnaming it is found in the fact that God (may He be exalted) had commanded that everything good should be offered upon it, beginning from Abel, see Genesis 4:4, "And Able offered, also, of the firstlings of his sheep and of its fat ones" This mountain offering corresponds with the written traditions kept by this people. God (may He be exalted) commanded it, namely, that everything good and holy should be offered to Him upon this mountain. We find the following in Deuteronomy 12:11, "To the place which the Lord your God shall choose from your tribes to cause his name to dwell there; ye shall bring thither what I am commanding you" as far as "and the best of the vows ye vow to God."

10. The tenth name is "THE CHOSEN PLACE," as in verse 5 of the same chapter, and in many other passages.

11. The eleventh name is "THE HIGHEST IN THE WORLD." So called it our two great lords, our lord Jacob and our lord Moses (upon them be peace), in blessing they gave Joseph (upon whom be peace). The words of our lord Jacob (upon whom be peace) are as follows: He said in the blessing. "The blessings of thy father and of thy mother have prevailed upon the blessing of the mountains." Again, "Even to the bound of the highest in the world" shall be to the chief Joseph (upon whom be peace). Our lord Moses (upon whom be peace) spoke in blessing Joseph (upon whom be peace) as follows: "From the best things of the ancient mountain and the best things of the highest in the world." He meant that this mountain is the highest of the earth's mountains in point of excellency and altitude.

12. The twelfth name is "THE FIRST OF MOUNTAINS," situated within the boundaries of the best of the tribes. Compare what God (may He be exalted) said about it to our lord Abraham (upon whom be peace): "Upon the best, or first, of mountains, which I will tell you." This was when God (may He be exalted) was trying his allegiance by commanding him to offer his son Isaac (upon whom be peace), as in Genesis 22:2, "Take thy son, thy only son, whom thou lovest, Isaac, and bring him to the land of *Moreh* and offer him as an offering upon the first of mountains, which I will tell you."

13. The thirteenth name is "GOD IS SEEN." It was given by our lords Abraham and Moses (upon them be peace). Compare Genesis 22:14.

14. The fourteenth name is "THE MOUNTAIN OF THE INHERITANCE OF THE SHEKINAH," for our lord Moses (upon whom be peace) said: "In the mountain of thy inheritance, the place of thy dwelling," as we have previously explained in this chapter.

Both the Samaritan and Jewish copies agree that our lord Joshua (upon whom be peace), before his death, gathered all Israel, and they stood in the presence of God in the tabernacle, as we read in the Jewish book of Joshua, chapter 24.

He made there a covenant with them that should remain faithful to the keeping of the Law, given through our lord Moses, the son of Amram (upon whom be peace). Just after that it is said, "And he made them a statute and an ordinance in Shechem," the city now known as Nablus. That was immediately before his death.

To prove what we have said, let it be known that Nablus was the capital of the kingdom of Israel, and one of its mountains was Mount Gerizim, whereupon, during the life of our lord Joshua (upon whom be peace), the tabernacle was erected. Another proof is that all those, who served in the tabernacle, namely, Eleazer, Phinehas, Ithamar, Shisha, Bahka and Uzza and the seventy elders, who prophesied from the gift of our lord Moses (upon whom be peace), all of these were ordered to be buried opposite the aforesaid mountain, and so it was done. They were buried opposite the noble mountain in Amarta, after they had spent their age in serving in the tabernacle. Their graves are still known to both Samaritans and Jews unto this day. If, according to the fancy of the Jews, the tabernacle had been in Jebus, these great priests would have been buried there. One sees their graves all directed towards this mountain.

Thus do the Samaritans prove their sanctuary the true plan of prayer, appealing not to their own traditions only, but to the testimony of priests whom the Jews also honor, whose graves, now with us and undisputed, bear their own eloquent testimony to the truth which we profess, for those graves point, as we pray, toward the Holy Mountain, where we still worship the God of our fathers.

Let me conclude this chapter by saying: this is the creed of the Samaritans and their belief in this mountain. They offer their sacrifices upon it, and perform upon it all that is necessary for their sanctification, in accordance with Deuteronomy 33:18-19. They argue that the prophet-leader, who shall lead the world, will surely appear. He will bring up again the Shekinah upon the aforesaid mountain, in the second kingdom, when God shall look with favor upon his people and shall forgive them.

O GOD, DIRECT US TO THY PLEASURE, AND CONFIRM US IN THE BEST FAITH THROUGH THE INTERMEDIATION OF OUR LORD AND PROPHET MOSES, THE SON OF AMRAM!

THIS CHAPTER IS WHAT A TIRED MIND AND A WEAK INTELLIGENCE COULD ATTAIN WITHIN THE LIMITS OF BRIEFNESS.

AND GOD KNOWS BEST.

AMRAM SON OF ISAAC
CHEIF OF THE HIGHER COMMUNITY OF THE SAMARITAN RELIGION

Greek Convent Press — Jerusalem

THE BOOK OF ENLIGHTENMENT

FOR THE INSTRUCTION OF THE INQUIRER

By
JACOB, SON OF AARON

High Priest of the Samaritans at Nablous, Palestine

Translated from the Arabic by
PROFESSOR A. BEN KORI

Pacific University - Forest Grove, Oregon

Edited by
WILLIAM E. BARTON, D.D.
Pastor of the First Congregational Church, Oak Park, Ill.

The Puritan Press
Sublette, Ill. 1913

The chapters comprising this book were first printed in BIBLIOTHECA SACBA In 1913, following other important writings by the Samaritan High Priest. The courtesy of the editor is acknowledged in their reprinting.

PRESS OF
THE NEWS PRINTING COMPANY
OBERLIN, OHIO

PREFATORY NOTE

This book is printed by the generosity of Mr. E. K. Warren, an American friend of the Samaritans, and is furnished to the High Priest in order that its sale may afford a small revenue for the Samaritan colony. These people are very poor, and tourists who wish to assist in the maintenance of the school can do so by the purchase of this and other books for sale by them.

The editor desires to ask American tourists visiting Palestine to make their purchases of Samaritan books as directly as possible from the priests at Nablous (Shechem). Spurious manuscripts are for sale by dealers and others. The High Priest guarantees that all copies of the Samaritan books sold at the Synagogue are correct and entire, and that the proceeds go to the school.

Throughout many centuries this singular little sect has continued to live under the shadow of its holy mountain. Some good purpose, surely, God will yet reveal through their existence. This book, which is curious and interesting, will assist to a correct understanding of their life and teaching.

-THE EDITOR

INTRODUCTORY NOTE

The following work was prepared, at the request of the editor, by the Samaritan High Priest, and is designed to answer the questions which are most frequently asked of the Samaritan priests, both by strangers and by some of their own communion. He has entitled the book "The Book of Enlightenment for the Instruction of the Inquirer." It is written in Arabic in neat manuscript, the quotations from Scripture being in the Samaritan Hebrew, and written in red ink.

It cannot be pretended that the questions are in every case those that the average American scholar is most eager to propose. But the book as a whole is not only interesting but instructive. It is a succinct statement of the present tenets of the Samaritans, and a fine example of their dialectic. The attention of scholars is increasingly directed to the Samaritans for the valuable side light which their customs throw on many questions of Jewish practice. The editor believes that this is a permanently valuable document.

The questions which the High Priest undertakes to answer are the following:

1. Concerning the duration of the plagues of Egypt. His answer is that the whole time covered by the plagues, including the intervals between them, was two months and a half.

2. Concerning the number and classification of the miracles. He counts the number as eleven, holding that the sign of the rod in the hand of Moses should be counted a sign in itself, in addition to the specific miracles wrought by it, in the plagues. He classifies the miracles as those wrought by God alone, those wrought by God through Moses, those wrought through Aaron, and those in which both Moses and Aaron were employed.

3. Concerning the origin and significance of the ceremonial year. He holds that the new calendar established at the time of the Exodus was really the reestablishment of the calendar begun at the creation.

4. Concerning the time of the institution of the Passover. This leads him into a full discussion of all that is involved in the Passover, and incidentally brings in the condemnation of a heretic who taught that the prohibition of fire which belongs to the Sabbath does not apply to the Passover. This heretic, who is nameless here, lived in 1753 A.D. But he did not succeed in gaining converts, even his own wife deserting his teaching; and the priest offers a prayer for his restoration, though he would appear to have been long dead.

5. Concerning the Passover when the date falls on the Sabbath. The answer is that, in this case, the sacrifice must take place on Friday, after sunset. To this answer he appends proof that Mount Gerizim is the one place where this sacrifice should be offered.

6. Concerning the forty years in the wilderness. The answer is that the ordinances of the Passover, Circumcision, and the Shekinah were faithfully observed.

7. Concerning the fasts of Moses. The answer is that Moses fasted for three periods of forty days each, and not merely two such periods.

8. Concerning the writing of the Commandments. The answer is that the Commandments were written for the sake of verbal accuracy and permanent preservation, and the greater reverence paid to a certain word of God, which might have been lost or corrupted if transmitted orally.

9. Concerning the revelation of the Torah. The answer, given at great length and with wide variety of proof, is that the complete Torah was written in a single roll by the hand of God, and came down to Moses complete. The apparent exceptions are noted, and

the main proposition is established by seven proofs.

10. Concerning the two stone tablets. The answer is that the first set of two tablets was created by God on the third day of creation. The inscription was in horizontal lines and in uncial characters. The writing miraculously disappeared when Moses broke the stones; the breaking of them if the writing had remained would have been either impossible or a great sin. The second set Moses hewed out, but God wrote on them. The size was as follows: length, one and a half cubits; breadth, three fourths of a cubit, combined thickness, two and one half cubits, completely filling the ark.

11. Concerning the tablets of testimony. The answer is that the stone tablets were called the tablets of testimony because they were a living testimony and covenant, testifying both the will of God and the promise of his people.

12. Concerning the transcription of the Torah. The answer is that the written Torah was given to Moses between the two sets of tablets containing the Commandments, and was copied by Moses and the priests. Whether the original copy, written directly by God, was ever taken out of the tent, where Joshua guarded it, is disputed. Some hold that it was exhibited once in seven years. The two copies made by Moses were all that were commonly seen.

13. Concerning the Jordan. The answer is that the Jordan is the river of Law. There the manna ceased, and the Law became fully operative.

14. Concerning the shining of Moses' face. The answer is that this phenomenon - the more remarkable because Moses had been fasting for forty days - was due to the effulgence of the angel Gabriel, who, without the knowledge of Moses, lent him his own presence and celestial brightness.

15. Concerning the water at Rephidim. The answer is that the

smiting of the rock was an authentication of Moses, and a rebuke to those who complained.

16. Concerning the battle with the Amalekites. The answer is that this was a testimony to the nations of the favor of Jehovah for his people Israel.

17. Concerning the reason for not destroying the Amalekites earlier. In order that Israel might know that its strength was in Jehovah. In this connection the High Priest goes outside the Torah, and, quoting from "the book attributed to Joshua," refers to the stopping of the sun as an event of this campaign. The battle occurred on Friday, he explains, and the standing of the sun was to preserve the Sabbath unbroken by the battle.

18. Concerning the time of Jethro's visit. It occurred in the second year of the Exodus.

19. Concerning the sons of Moses. They returned with their mother and their descendants still live, nomads, but monotheists. In this connection the High Priest refutes the slander against Moses, that, after the departure of Zipporah, Moses married a negress. Against the Jews, to whom the priest attributes this slander, he cries, "May God fight them for this!" The woman, he says, was none other than Zipporah herself, and the word does not mean "black" but "beautiful."

20. Concerning the heir of an adulteress. The high priest, who condemns her to death, inherits her property.

21. Concerning the face of Laban. Jacob read the heart of Laban in his face, and knew that he was in disfavor. The face reveals the heart.

22. Concerning Oaths. The High Priest classifies these, with some elaboration, into oaths permissible and prohibited; the prohibited oaths are of three kinds those of falsehood, conjecture, or triviality; and the permissible, those that affirm

truthfully and reverently.

23. Concerning the inheritance of a woman who marries outside the tribe. Her inheritance remains to her heirs within the tribe. It is forfeited so far as she, her husband, and her children are concerned.

24. Concerning the use of rennet. The prohibition of seething a kid in its mother's milk had not been carried, so far as the High Priest knows, to the point of forbidding the use of the kid's stomach in the making of cheese. When attention was called to this, however, he investigated the matter; and while he could find no question of this particular in the literature of his people, it seemed to him clear that the use of rennet was a violation of the Law, so he has prohibited it, establishing a new precedent. In this, however, he does not condemn those who preceded him, as what they did in violation of the Law in this regard was done inadvertently.

25. Concerning the abridgment by laymen of the authority of the priesthood. Some laymen having insisted that there should be a group of lay associates with the priests to pass upon questions where the rights of the priesthood are involved, the High Priest refutes their claim, showing that the laity have no right to intermeddle in matters of this character, and incidentally showing with how great respect the high priest himself ought to be treated.

The High Priest closes by hurling two questions at those who oppose him. The first is, that they will explain the command not to remove the ancient landmark. The second is, that they explain the command "Thou shalt love thy neighbor as thyself." With these two arguments one against the method and the other against the spirit of those who oppose him, the High Priest closes the book.

-WILLIAM E. BARTON.

THE BOOK OF ENLIGHTENMENT

In the name of the Most Merciful God, in whom is my trust. At some previous times, on many occasions, members of my own tribe have asked me questions, the solution of which was hidden from them, because of the scarcity of books to guide them. I have answered these inquiries from time to time in accordance with the best efforts of my weak mind and poor understanding. I have wished also to record the substance of these answers, both for safekeeping, and for the benefit of following generations. I pray God for his help. Amen.

  Praise be to God, the quintessence of Unity; the indivisible and eternal;
  To him who is far above either mother or son;
  To the forgiver of sins to everyone that repents with purity of conscience;
  To him who overlooks shortcomings, and consoles the disconsolate hearts;
  To him who alone is perfect and eternal, and liable neither to malady nor disease.
  He is eternal and immutable, far above destruction, or any possible damage.
  He is the Everlasting, who is too exalted to be represented either by image or likeness,
  And is far above measurement or drawing.
  He is described by the most exalted names;
  To him belongs the ineffable name "AHIH ASHR AHIH."
  He is the one who hears and beholds all things.
  Verily he hears the flowing of water in the most parched wilderness,
  And sees the black ants in the darkest recesses of the rock.
  There is no God but be;
  None but he is worthy to be worshiped.
  He is invisible, eternal in his eternity,
  And Lord of all the heavens.

Exalted and blessed be his Name!
He is praised in the secret and in the open;
In the conscience and by the tongue;
Inwardly and outwardly.
He is the only judge,
Who will avenge himself on the rebellious on the last day.
Holy be his great name! Amen.

I. THE DURATION OF THE PLAGUES OF EGYPT

I have been asked, concerning the wonders which took place with respect to Pharaoh and his people, How long did each and all of the plagues last? The answer is as follows:

As to the period during which the wonders took place by the hand of our lord, the apostle Moses (upon whom be peace), while he was in Egypt, it was that of two months and a half.

The first wonder took place in the eleventh month, and the last took place in the first. It is so affirmed by our traditions, handed down from father to son, and is so accepted and agreed upon by the people of Israel.

We believe that the wonder of the staff that turned into a serpent lasted less than a single day. As to the wonder of blood, it lasted seven days; for we read: "And seven days were fulfilled after Jehovah had smitten the river." The period of the wonder of frogs lasted two days. That of the plague of lice is not mentioned. Some assert that the plague; has continued on Egypt ever since that day.

The plague of flies lasted only one day, and left them on the day following. The miracle of the destruction of the cattle lasted only one hour. As to the wonder of the boils with blains, it lasted a whole week. The miracle of the hail lasted one day; likewise lasted the plague of locusts. The miracle of darkness lasted three days, as we read: "For a period of three days no man saw his brother." The period of the killing of the first-born lasted one single hour. To one who might make the statement that these periods would not make out the total time of two and one half months, as previously indicated, the answer is, that there transpired some intervals of time between one miracle and another. It is asserted that the time divisions were uniform, and that each was of seven days, including the period of each miracle and the interval; for, as soon as the miracle of blood ceased, the Nile let loose on them its frogs, and the whole earth was filled with them. However, a certain amount of space elapsed after each miracle, that the two apostles might have time to carry their message to Pharaoh and to receive his reply thereto, and act accordingly.

Thus the whole period of miracles amounted to two months and a half.

And God possesses the best knowledge of all things.

II. THE NUMBER AND CLASSIFICATION OF THE MIRACLES

The next question is concerning the meaning of the words "Pharaoh shall not listen to you."

The first purpose of this prediction is in order that the words of God may be confirmed; namely, "Pharaoh shall not listen to you, and I will produce my power upon the Egyptians." It was God's purpose that Pharaoh should know and feel, together with his people, these signs and wonders while he was still hardened in his unbelief.

Secondly, that these miracles might be a warning to those who should come later on. Otherwise it would have been possible for God to destroy Pharaoh with his people in the twinkling of an eye. In fact, God desired by this prediction and his delay to show the greatness of his apostle and the veracity of his statements; he therefore performed these astounding wonders through him as a memorial to all the generations, in order that the one who reads them, and meditates on them, may continue in his fidelity to him and consider and fear the treacherous unbeliever. He made us know, therefore, that the unwillingness of Pharaoh to hearken unto his two messengers resulted in what he said, "that my miracles may be multiplied in the land of Egypt." The genuineness of the mission of these two men was proved; for we read: "and Moses and Aaron performed all these miracles" (Exodus 11:10). There exist among the learned men some who claim that these miracles amounted to ten in number, thus omitting from their reckoning the miracle of the staff which was turned into a serpent. Some say that the latter is only a sign, and not a miracle. But those who claim that the number of miracles is ten do unconsciously prove it to be twenty, for, according to them, the happening of the miracle is miraculous and its disappearance is also miraculous.

It is more correct, however, to count them as eleven miracles, for the matter of the staff was both a sign and a miracle, according to the statement of God: "Show me a sign," or a miracle (Exodus 7:9); for a sign is in itself a miracle. This statement is proved by the words of God, which have already been quoted (Exodus 11:10), which verse includes all the miracles that have transpired. The same is affirmed by more than one of God's statements, as in the same chapter and verse, "and God hardened the heart of Pharaoh; he neither hearkened unto them nor let the people depart from his land."

These miracles include within themselves many others, the details of which are lengthy and numerous. Here are, however, some of the principal divisions.

(1) The bringing of the flies, murrain, and the killing of the first-born. These are the direct doings of God, without the instrumentality of the two apostles. It must be understood, however, that the message which accompanied these wonders was delivered by Moses, who, with his brother, knew about them.

(2) Those which were done by God by the hand of Moses alone, while Aaron had simply to notify Pharaoh with the words of his brother. They are the hail, the locusts, and the darkness. These were done simply by Moses, and Aaron had part only in the intercession which accompanied them.

(3) Those which God performed by the hand of Aaron, while Moses had only to give the command. They are the turning of the staff into a serpent, the miracle of frogs, and that of lice.

(4) Those in which both brothers took part. They are the turning of water into blood, and the boils.

But the real agent of them all was indeed God (who is highly exalted). He only used these two apostles to prove the truthfulness of their message, and to show forth their high character and standing, and that the rest of the world might know, as we have already stated. The line found in Exodus 11:9 does simply indicate to us that there were performed ten wonders on Pharaoh; and that, in spite of their bitterness and hardship, in spite of the tortures which he suffered therefrom, he did not let the children of Israel depart from his land except after the killing of the first-born, which wonder makes the eleventh. Compare Exodus 7:3, "And I will... multiply my signs and my wonders in the land of Egypt. But Pharaoh will not hearken unto you until I lay my hand on Egypt, and bring out my hosts, my people the children of Israel, from the land of Egypt." The laying of his hand does not refer to the killing of the first-born: "And I will stretch forth my hand, and smite Egypt with all my wonders which I shall perform in the midst of it. Thereupon he shall let you depart" (Exodus 3:20). This verse refers to the performance of all the wonders. And to God belongs the best knowledge.

III. THE ORIGIN AND SIGNIFICANCE OF THE CEREMONIAL YEAR

I have been asked, concerning the passage "This month shall be to you the beginning of months" (Exodus 12:2), Did the Israelites know, previous to this statement, that this month was the first month of their year, or did they begin so to look on it afterwards? The following is in answer. And my success comes from God.

Yes, they knew it as the first month from ancient times; for, in the account of the deluge (Genesis 8:13), we read: "In the six hundredth and first year and the first month, on the first day of the month," etc. The same mention is given in Exodus 7:2, in order that the noble and exalted nature of the month might be shown, and that we might know that the delivery of the children of Israel from Egypt's bondage took place thereon. There is, however, a stronger reason. It is called the first month of the year, that we may thereby find with exactness the various times of the year which we are commanded to observe, and as such they are called the days of fulfillment of righteousness. During the same, on well-known periods we have our festival days. Compare the reference given in Exodus 7:3, "Speak to the congregation of Israel, saying, that on the tenth of this month, they shall take for themselves each a sheep," etc. Read as far as the sixth verse, wherein it is said, "and it shall be kept by you until the fourteenth of this month." From these references we conclude that this month was the first, and with it the year begins; that on the tenth day of the same month sacrificial offerings are to be chosen and kept till the close of the fourteenth day. The sacrifices should take place on the evening of the night of the fifteenth of the month. Beginning with that day up to the twenty-first, unleavened bread must be eaten for seven days; and that day, which is the twenty-first, must be spent in the service of God. In this manner the arrangement of festival days was made out, each according to his time and month, as their order is given in the Book of the Law; and that is why the month is called the first.

As to the command that the celebration of the Passover on its proper times should take place to the end of generations, it is because the offerings of Passover during the days of Darkness are equivalent to those of the entire year. They are equivalent to the peace offerings. To continue to celebrate the same will lead us to the days of the appearance of God's Pleasure and the coming of the second prophet. The mystery which affirms God's Pleasure, falling as it does in this month, will doubtless be approved to us that the return of God's Pleasure will be during the same month, namely, the first. As to the command of God in reference to the celebration of the Passover in its time, one is referred to Exodus 12:17, "Ye shall observe and fulfill this day in your generations as an eternal ordinance"; "Ye shall keep this command as an eternal ordinance to thee and to thy children" (verse 24). Again: "Thou shall keep this ordinance in its time from year to year" (Exodus 13:10). Compare also Deuteronomy 16:1, "Keep the month of Abib." Thus it appears that the month of Abib is the first month, corresponding to April. The keeping of this month is simply for giving praise and thanks to God for having saved them from the servitude of the Egyptians. They should also continue to mention the reason for God's action in bringing them out of Egypt. See, therefore, Deuteronomy 16:12, "and remember also that thou wert a slave in the land of Egypt." As to the usefulness of celebrating this ordinance from year to year as the ages pass, it consists in blotting out the sins of each year as long as it is kept on the first month, which is April, when occur the return of God's Pleasure and the reappearance and reestablishment of the Shekinah on Mount Gerizim. As to the time and place, both are proved by the word of God. The Shekinah was established in the wilderness by Moses on the first month, and when our lord Joshua (upon whom be peace) set it up on Mount Gerizim, it was on the first month. Its return will be by the will of God on the first month. And that is the reason why God commanded and declared the keeping of its season. As to the place, it shall be in the chosen place, the place whose selection was revealed after their entrance into the Holy Land. No other place shall be substituted for it: only in it and within its boundaries. In proof of the same, compare Deuteronomy 16:5, "It shall not be lawful unto thee to sacrifice the Passover within any of the towns," etc.; and: "But it must be in the place which the Lord thy God has chosen that his name may dwell there. There shalt thou sacrifice the Passover in the evening at sunset," etc. This place is Mount Gerizim. And God knows all things.

IV. THE TIME OF THE INSTITUTION OF THE PASSOVER

Were the apostles Moses and Aaron given the ordinance of the Passover, and the manner of its performance, on the first day of the first month, or on some other of its days previous to the fourteenth?

There is a variety of opinions given by the learned men. Some claim that the probability is that the command was given on the first of the month, with the provision that on the tenth they should choose the offerings and keep them under surveillance until the evening of the fourteenth. During these days the offerings would have been washed daily, and cleansed and purified from all the blemishes and forms of animal filth until the Egyptians were assured that Israel was ready to offer them to his God. Their intention was revealed during this period of four days, and the Egyptians could not pretend that the Israelites had sacrificed their offerings in a concealed manner. There are others who claim that the command was given by God only on the fourteenth of April, on the day known to us as *Alfajool*. In proof of the same compare Exodus 11:4, "In the midst of the night I will go out into the midst of the land of Egypt." Pharaoh, who realized that every threatening made to him by the apostle Moses (upon whom be peace) would be fulfilled, placed guards around his own first-born prince, lest he should perish with the first-born of the Egyptians. Naturally he commanded them to watch over his son without remittance, and not to sleep throughout the whole night. The guards were probably men of trust, famous for their courage and daring, and they obeyed the command of Pharaoh with all diligence. While they were in the most careful act of watchfulness over the first-born of Pharaoh, behold the latter was dead in the midst of them, while they were around him and without having noticed anyone entering among them. These words belong to the high priest Merkah (may God's pleasure be upon him). Amen.

Now if anyone should say that, if God's command was given on the fourteenth of the month, he would not have said, also, "on the tenth of this month," in reply to this question it must be said that the words of God here form a part of the ordinance of the Passover, and they were a command to those of the coming generations, for he said also: "That which remaineth of it until morning shall be burned in fire" (Exodus 12:10); while they did not remain in Egypt, but rather got up early and left in all haste.

Now the reconciliation of this command of the Passover in a year when it shall fall on the Sabbath will be given in its time, if God will help.

The learned elder, of blessed memory, Ishmael Arrabjee, mentioned in his book named "Hitoroth," that is to say, Legislation, informs us that the command of the Lord to the two apostles took place on the day known to us as the day of Alfajool, while they were still in Egypt on the night of the Passover. Thus our learned men differ. And God possesses the best knowledge.

This book became extinct in the twelfth century, because none took care of it in those days. Part of it is still with the writer, and another part with some of the Samaritan people. If God will grant me the required years I shall gather what can be found according to my ability. It contains *Toroot* and *Mosoot*, and possesses some fine interpretations. These words belong to my uncle, the generous and literary sheik Shamsu Deen Sadkah. May God grant him forgiveness; for it is a very interesting book. And the knowledge of the unknown belongs to God.

Remarks concerning the Ordinance of the Passover

Our people who dwell in the villages and countries which are more or less remote from the Chosen Place used to sacrifice the offerings of the Passover where they lived. We know also, from verified reports, that in those days a party that belonged to the Chosen Place used to burn large fires upon the top of Mount

Gerizim, that those living in the adjacent countries, such as Askelon, and Caesarea, and other towns, might see the same and act accordingly. Those who came and sacrificed in the Chosen Place were permitted to sacrifice either sheep or oxen, but those who sacrificed in other places were not permitted to sacrifice, except sheep. But in our generation, and in past ones beginning from a period of three hundred years ago, it has been agreed that offerings shall be made nowhere except on the Chosen Place, or if the mountain itself should ever become impossible, then on its slope or in places as near to it as practicable.

This is to harmonize with the saying of God in Deuteronomy 16:5, "It shall not be lawful unto thee to sacrifice the Passover within any of thy gates, (that is, in towns) which the Lord thy God has given thee, but only in the Place which the Lord thy God has chosen, that his name might dwell therein. There shalt thou sacrifice the Passover."

Again, the custom has not varied from ancient times until the present (that is, from the period of two hundred years ago until now), that only sheep, and none else, shall be used for sacrifices. In our days it has been agreed to choose only the sheep of white color, because that is the color of the best and the noblest of the sheep. He who lives in any other place beyond the boundaries of the Chosen Place must hasten to the Chosen Place, and there sacrifice the Passover. Should he be late in coming without having any legal cause to delay him, he commits a great sin, and becomes liable to what God ordered in Numbers 9:13, "If a man be clean, and does not make a journey, and has failed to sacrifice the Passover, that soul shall be cut off from among the people; for he has not sacrificed to God in season. That man shall bear his own sins." If a man asks, "How can a man bear his own sins if he has been cut off from his own people?", and, "Did he not pay for his sins by having been killed?", the answer is, that since his action was intentional, his sins will be counted against him till the day of vengeance, when, in the day of judgment and account, he shall be compelled to render an account of his sins and shall be punished for them. His killing became necessary both because he has offended his Lord, and also in order that others in this world may be led to consider and not transgress likewise.

Questions of this character are numerous in the Law. Among the conditions of the Passover is that the sacrifices shall be chosen on the tenth of the month and kept with diligence until the time of their offering, according to the command of God in Exodus 12:3, etc.: "On the tenth of this month they shall take for themselves every man a lamb according to the houses of their fathers, a lamb for every house; and if the house be too small for a lamb, the family shall join in company with its neighbor who lives nearest to his house according to the numbers of souls," etc., to the line where it is said, "the same shall be kept until the fourteenth day of the month." During these five days the sacrifices must be examined, and the condition of the animals found out, lest they have same of the objections to disqualify them, such as blisters, which is characteristic of the sheep, or a redness of eye, or a possibly fatal disease. Their hoofs must be cleansed; especially those parts which grow within the hoofs, for they are liable to much dirt, and whatever defects they may be found to possess disqualify them from being sacrificed. A sheep is particularly disqualified by such a blemish as a break in the leg or defect in sight. All their members should be cleansed from dirt; for they tread upon the defiled things while walking in the streets and highways. Occasionally there grow between their hoofs diseased parts which disqualify them.

Every Israelite must be taxed according to his share with the cost of those sacrifices to fulfill the command of the Lord, "According to their souls' price;" and this command includes all, the man and the woman and the child. Anyone who is not taxed, and does not pay out of his own material substance, cannot have sacrifices. But he who is too poor, and does not possess anything in this world, may serve in the preparation of the sacrifices, and substitute his labor for money, and thus make up what he would have been taxed as his share. And if a man lives with a family, and has always been looked upon as a member of it, he may pay the taxes that will cover all its members, whether they be wife, child, or servants, in accordance with the words of God found in Exodus 12:4, "If the house, however, has no one to pay the full price, it may join with its nearest neighbor, and the price be divided in accordance with the number of those who partake of the sacrifice." This, of course, was in the days of the large growth and multitude of the Israelites, but when their conditions changed for the worse, and their number decreased exceedingly, a number of them, large or small, would agree and undertake to procure their sacrifices as they saw fit. But nowadays, on account of our present condition, and on account of our small number, we make a common fund of the little we possess. We all gather together into one company and have one furnace, and this has been done for nearly one hundred and twenty-five years. This we do because of our weakness and ill prosperity, and on account of the days of darkness. It is not permissible for anyone to sacrifice except with his own relations. Of course the married woman, wherever she is, will sacrifice with her husband and will eat with him.

Among other ordinances is one that, on the fourteenth day, all the people of Israel should cleanse their houses and dwelling places, and clear them out entirely of leaven, according to Exodus 23:18, "Do not offer thy sacrifices with leavened bread, and let no fat of the Passover remain until morning." Therefore, the people of Israel agreed not to eat leavened bread on that day. Moreover, in order that any leaven previously eaten may have been digested thoroughly in the body, they eat not leavened bread on the fourteenth, lest they may violate the words of the Lord by eating it for eight days. Compare Exodus 12:18, "By an ordinance forever ye shall eat unleavened bread in the first month on the fourteenth day at even until the twenty-first at even." According to this command, seven days only must be completed.

Another condition is that none of the people of Israel should offer sacrifices unless he be pure in body, void of all defilements and their causes. He must not have the least reason of being defiled.

Another condition is that the whole people should gather

together, according to Exodus 12:6, "And the whole company of the children of Israel should kill it at evening," that they all may witness the offerings of God, and all may remember his favors upon them and upon their forefathers, and the signs and wonders which he performed for them, their delivery from servitude.

This remembrance is necessary. Compare Exodus 12:14, "It shall be a memorial unto you this day." Compare also what Moses said, "Remember also this day" (Exodus 13:3). Much can be said in reference to these commands.

During the celebration of the Passover the people must indulge greatly in praises, in exultations and glorifications, and must not cease doing so throughout the whole night; for it is called the Night of God. Compare, with others, Exodus 12:42, "This night belongs to God; it shall be kept by the children of Israel in all their generations."

Another condition is that the offering should be sacrificed at evening, not before and not after. It must be done as the sun goes under, that it may have a well-defined demarcation. As to our custom when the Passover falls on the Sabbath, it will be explained later on, by God's Word.

Another condition is, that the sacrifice which is offered must be examined internally, lest it may have broken bones, or weak lungs, or any internal disease.

Another condition is that all its fat, including the two kidneys, must be taken away, for if any of these remain with it, it cannot be offered. The right shoulder, together with the fat, must be removed, before it can be broiled with the meat.

Another condition is that it must be broiled thoroughly in fire. There is no question about the verse in Deuteronomy 16:7. It does not imply that the meat should be cooked with water, for the command has already been given that it should not be eaten raw or boiled. See Exodus 12:8-9, "Do not eat any part of it raw or cooked with water."

Another condition is that it must be salted according to the common taste. It must not be eaten without salt. Compare Leviticus 2:13, "With all thine oblations thou shall offer salt."

Another condition is that it must be eaten in the middle of the night, and all those who partake of it must do so in the guise of men who are about to go on a journey and are prepared for travel. They must be girded in the middle; must have their leather shoes on their feet, and their staves in their hands, according to Exodus 12:11, "Thus shall ye eat it. Your loins must be girded, your sandals must be on your feet and your staves in your hands." In other words, in eating it the triumph and joy of the Exodus may be celebrated, for it is a Passover and a salvation from the oppression in which our forefathers found themselves: "Ye shall eat it greedily, for it is a Passover to God." Thus they would remember the departure of the forefathers from Egypt. They ate it while on the point of departure, and they ate it with greediness, on account of the anxiety caused by the impending journey: "For haste hast thou left Egypt: that thou mayest remember thy departure out of the land of Egypt all the days of thy life" (Deuteronomy 16:3).

Another condition is that it must be eaten with unleavened bread and bitter herbs. As to the eating of it with unleavened bread, it is to remind them of the state of oppression and poverty and difficulty in which they were while in Egypt; for unleavened bread was called, in another place, *lehem eneh*, that is, "the bread of the poor." For often the poor, and those on the point of a long journey on account of their poverty, haste, or hunger, would take the flour, and knead it and bake it all at once, and eat it in haste without waiting for it to be leavened. The traveler may do likewise from his haste or the anxiety which he feels. He may become impatient should he wait until it becomes leavened. But God possesses the best knowledge.

As to the eating of bitter herbs, it is that they may remember also the bitter lives which their forefathers lived, the oppressive servitude and the excessive tasks with which they were cumbered. As to the making of unleavened bread, it must be done with all carefulness lest any foreign matter be mixed with it. It must be selected from the whole amount of wheat chosen for the season. It must be cleansed, especially at its grinding at the mill; it must not be gathered up out of the wheat which has been threshed by oxen, for while they are drawing the threshing instrument they might defile it by their urine and dung. Compare Leviticus 22:25, "Neither from the hand of a foreigner shall ye offer the bread of your God of any of these, because their corruption is in them; there is a blemish in them; they shall not be accepted for you." Now if there is no wheat of which the conditioned portion can be taken; if there be no Israelite farmers from whom the required amount can be taken, ears of wheat must be picked at the time of harvest and preserved until it can be prepared for the making of unleavened bread.

Another condition is that the lamb must be roasted entirely as a whole, with its head and its legs, without any part being cut off, except the right shoulder, which is removed that the same may be eaten afterward, being the property of the priests, the sons of Levi. Compare Exodus 12:9, "Its head with its legs and the inwards thereof."

Another condition is that it must not be taken out from the place where it is cooked; it must not be taken from one place to another: "Thou shalt not carry forth aught of the flesh 'brought out of the house'" (Exodus 12:46), lest it may undergo some disqualification, or lest it may be changed. No bone of it shall be broken. "Neither shall ye break the bones thereof."

Another condition is that no foreigner shall touch it, and no foreigner shall eat of it except him who possesses the religion of Israel and has been circumcised and purified. If a slave bought by money has been converted, and has taken up our religion and has been circumcised, he may eat of it; he may sacrifice it as any of the Israelites, according to Exodus 12:44, "But every man's servant who is bought for money, when thou hast circumcised him, then shall he eat thereof."

Now as to strangers, our Law says (in the same chapter, verse 48): "When a stranger shall sojourn with thee and will keep the Passover of Jehovah, if he be a male, let him be circumcised; then he shall be as one born in the land." This statement includes any one, whether he be stranger or not, who has taken up this religion and introduced himself under the ordinances of the Law. He who does that, let it be announced to him that his standing before God and in the house of the Lord is like the standing of the Israelite. For he said in the same chapter, "He shall be like a native in the land, for he has submitted himself and restrained his passions unto the will of God. Let him therefore be fruitful."

Another condition is that its fat must be burned, and whatever fatness may be found in the head and in the shoulder, and whatever may remain of the flesh and bones and members, without leaving a particle of it, in accordance with the command of God in Exodus 12:10, "Leave nothing of it until the morning."

Every Israelite must cease working that he may have a part in the offering of the sacrifice. The least work must not be done, and he who excludes the preparation of food in general, claiming that it can be done on the day of the Passover, he has surely ignored the word of God, for if any work were intended besides that of the Passover the word "only" or "singly" would not have been employed. For this work does surely refer to the Passover only, and therefore the taking part in the Passover is the only thing that can be done at the prescribed time, in accordance with the command of God. If, however, the objector of these explanations would suggest that God, in saying "for every soul," meant that whatever may be eaten may be prepared on the day of the Passover, but must not be eaten except by the Israelite who is pure, the answer is, that God had this command only for the children of Israel, and if he had simply said, "Whatever may be eaten by every soul may be prepared," we might be convinced.

But since he added a conditional word, which is *lbdo*, namely, "only" or "singly," and concluded his saying by the word *lkm*, that is, "to you," it follows that he meant the Passover, and that they alone were responsible for its observance. And to God belongs the highest wisdom.

If, however, someone may say that the preparation of the Passover is simply limited to a day, but not the preparation of other food God meant for two days, namely, that day of the Passover and the day of the Feast of Unleavened Bread, he is surely mistaken; for the saying of Jehovah referred only to the day of the Passover. Yes, God said that the least doing must not be done in them, namely, in those two days, but he made an additional remark in Exodus 12:16, which surely refers to the Passover only. The duty of every Israelite should be to be diligent and watchful lest something disqualifying might happen to his sacrifice.

Another condition is that early in the morning the whole host shall rise and depart to their places and homes. Compare Deuteronomy 16:7, "Then in the morning go to and leave for thy tents." The duty of every Israelite is, that he should make known the joy of the Passover in his home, and should bless God for the salvation of his forefathers from their enemies; and for the standing, the high standing, which is only his; and for the help by which he has been enabled to fulfill his Passover duty, especially in the days of darkness; for the absence of harm done him by his enemies; and for the liberty given him in preparing his sacrifice. Such things must be attributed to God's mercy and favor, and should be looked upon as the best guide to submission to this will. It is indeed a marvelous thing that, during the observance of the ordinance, none thinks of harming the Israelite, whether it be his body or his property. It is in assurance of the fulfillment of God's saying in Exodus 34:24, "No man shall desire thy land when thou goest up to appear before the Lord thy God." Let the Israelite watch over this holy day and cease from all works, in accordance with Exodus 12:16, "And the first day there shall be to you a holy convocation, and on the seventh day a holy convocation; no manner of work shall be done in them." This command is, of course, to include the Passover and the seventh day, which is the first of unleavened bread, "Save that which every man may eat, that alone may be done of you." This exception is made, referring to the Passover sacrifice and its preparation; and whatever may be needed to attend to the same is allowable. No other labor is permissible, and the Jewish people are in error in their claim, for they have taken this verse as intended for every feast in which they allow the cooking of all kinds of food. They have abandoned the ordinance, and perform things which are not mentioned in the holy Torah. They perform, however, the feast of unleavened bread, but only in part. The Gentiles claim that the Jews used blood, human blood, in their unleavened bread, which is, I believe, incorrect, and the report of a slanderer, for blood is a defiling thing with them as it is with us. And to God belongs the best wisdom.

But as to the ordinance of the Passover, the Jews have entirely neglected it, although it is an ordinance given to all generations forever. Compare Exodus 12:17, "Ye shall keep this ordinance, for on this very day I have brought your hosts out of the land of Egypt. Ye shall observe and fulfill this day throughout your generations." Let the reader answer, "What other day than on the day of the Passover did God bring the children of Israel out of Egypt?" And there can be no greater testimony of this fact than this line in Exodus 12:17, "Ye shall observe this ordinance."

It is plain enough that the words above refer to the Passover, and that all works on that day are unlawful, with the exception of the work which concerns the preparation of the Passover. For the command as to the prohibition of work on these two days was given before that of the Sabbath; and as the praiseworthy and highly exalted God wished to arrange for the rest of the annual feasts, he began with the commands concerning the feast of the Passover and ended with that of the eighth feast. He informed us that the standing of these feasts is as high as that of the Sabbath; for he often implied the Sabbath in mentioning the other festival days. Compare Leviticus 23:2, "The festival days of the Lord, ye shall call convocations of holiness, these are festival days." Such saying includes both the festival days and the Sabbath, for he has coupled the Sabbath with the festival days: "Six days shalt thou do work, but on the Sabbath there is a complete cessation of labor, a holy convocation. The least work ye shall not do; it is a rest day in your dwellings." Then he began mentioning the festival days in their order, and in the same manner the Sabbath; and as the Sabbath was devoted to God, likewise the rest of the festival days are devoted to him. Compare Leviticus 23:4, "These are the festivals of the Lord which ye shall call out in their seasons." Such a line is comprehensive, and the standing of the one festival is of equal importance.

The Condemnation of a Heresy as to the Use of Fire

What is wonderful in short-sighted and ignorant people who know little of the fullest import of the holy law is, that they claim that the feast of the Passover has nothing to do with the Sabbath, and does not have the obligations of the Sabbath. Thus one Israelite living outside of our own town in the year 1171 of the Hegira (1753 A.D.) did adopt a disgusting custom, and resolved upon making fire in his home during the festival days, claiming that fire is prohibited only on the Sabbath; as if, according to this theory, joy cannot be obtained except by making fire! Such persons are indeed ignorant; for, if joy is not obtained except through fire, the Sabbath had been worthier, in which the prohibition of fire is commanded. These words are taken from the learned sheik Mosallam Almoyan Addanafy, who erred therein, for the man who has given birth to such a deed is well nigh losing his religion. The reason for prohibiting the making of fire, on this, as on other festival days is that work need not be necessary. There is no exception which permits the making of fire in their homes. And that is why the revelation concerning the prohibition of fire was brought down just about the time the revelation concerning the building of the Shekinah was brought down. Before the apostle Moses (upon whom be peace) had given the tabernacle revelation, he gathered the whole people, and made them acquainted with the command of God concerning the keeping of the Sabbath and the prohibition of fire making. Compare Exodus 35:3, "Do not make any fire in all your dwellings on the day of the Sabbath." We know well what is meant by the word "day," namely, "from sunset to sunset." Compare Genesis 1:15; also Leviticus 23:32, "From sunset to sunset ye shall cease from work." Thus we know that by "day" we understand twenty-four hours, without paying attention to those who claim that the meaning of the "day" here is intended to imply only the period from sunrise to sunset, and excludes the night. After that revelation the apostle gave them the instruction concerning the building of the tabernacle. His insistence upon the total abstinence from making fire on it should be observed. The man who took upon himself the license of making fire upon the festival day was induced by his action to commit greater offenses; for, as I have read that this same heretic prepared on the festival day coffee for himself and drank it; he also smoked tobacco, and as this commodity brought about one of the principal confessions, he committed a great offense and transgressed the command of the Lord concerning all festival days: "Ye shall not do any work" (Leviticus 23:3). The action of that man caused him to do exactly what might defile him; for on the festival days he visited, and sat in conversation with, people of lewd character in cafes and the like, and associated with people who differed with him in religion. Like Haggoyim (the Gentiles) and others, instead of spending the day in the worship of God, he spent it in idleness, and in whatever might change and degrade the character of the day. He made himself like the Jews, who may justly be called by the aforesaid name for their deeds. All this was contrary to the sayings of God (whose Name is exalted) that on such days fulfillment of righteousness must be done. On such days our duties must be holy and pure; we must avoid all things that may reflect upon the day, and all defilements or anything that may have their shadows. We must be occupied in the worship of the exalted God, in reading his law and the like, which includes prayer, reading of appropriate portions, etc. This ignorant man, however, instead of sanctifying the day, defiled it. The elements of purity cannot be harmonized with those of impurity. Let it be known, therefore, that God (to whom be praise) prohibited us from doing any work on such days as are devoted to him, that he may fulfill righteousness on them by doing whatever is pure and holy, and by avoiding whatever may desecrate and defile us, that we who keep them may justly fulfill his sayings, "Ye shall be sanctified and be holy, for I am holy." Such days must be kept holy, and not defiled with works which may keep us away from worship, as is the case on the rest of the common days.

And thou, O ignorant and obstinate man, consider what great favor God bestowed upon his people Israel! He made them holy, set them apart, and preferred them above the rest, and gave them feasts which may claim a divine origin, and for a lawful purpose proceeding from the command of the Lord God (who is highly exalted) which sets definitely their times and seasons contrary to what may be found in another god. For no other god has instituted these festival days, nor is our God their author, but rather the god who made these customs is himself made by hands. Woe unto thee if thou wilt persist in this obstinacy and wilt refuse the heritage with which the Lord of Creation has endowed thee! Consider also what he has said about thee; about thy duty and about thy claim for him concerning the observance of his times, Leviticus 29:2, "Be ye holy for I am holy, the Lord your God;" also in chapter 26, "Be ye holy unto me, I am the Lord God who hath set you apart from the nations, that ye may be mine."

A most surprising thing, indeed, that persons who are well acquainted with the purpose of these statements may act contrary to them. If the ignorant may say, "I have done nothing; I have done only things which are commanded in the law, and if the prohibitions of making fire during the festival days were mentioned I would not have made fire," such a statement would confirm his ignorance and his persistence therein. For the command was not given to prohibit the making of fire, except that no work, not even the least, may be done, and there is no festival day, but a command in regard to it was given as follows: "Every work that is to be done thou shalt not do." About some of them he gave the following command in Leviticus 23:21, "Ye shall call on that very day a holy convocation for yourselves. The least work ye shall not do. It shall be an ordinance in your dwellings forever and to all generations," and if the festival days had something in addition to the days of the Sabbath, this day to which a reference is made by the same verse would be the most worthy of all, for God instituted the Sabbath as the day of "the short feast," and in that there is no difference between the Sabbath and the rest in so far as prohibiting work entirely; for he said about the Sabbath in Leviticus 23:3, "It is a Sabbath for the Lord in all your dwellings." He also said in Leviticus 23:21, "An ordinance forever in all your dwellings unto all your generations." The reference in the word *Moshbotekim* is to the making of fire, for works may take place either in the dwelling of man or outside of it, but the making of fire must necessarily take place within the dwelling. "Do not make fire in all your dwellings on the day of the Sabbath." In the references where the word *Moshbotekim* occurs, it is always given before *Dorotikim*, in order that all generations may know that this command has been given them beforehand, handed down from father to son as the time goes by; and whenever a new generation rises up, its houses may be seen void of fire on all the festival days, as on the Sabbath. New generations should do as those who preceded them in obedience to the command of God in Deuteronomy 32:7, "Ask thy father, and he will inform thee; the elders, and they will speak unto thee." This is exactly to answer any one who might confide in the heresy referred to above, without heeding the righteous truth, and following those who preceded him according to what they had handed him and what they themselves practiced, believing that his mind and knowledge are better than those of his ancestors. Such thinking as this is an additional proof of his stupendous ignorance and lack of knowledge, and of the scarcity of his understanding; for we have a proverb which runs as follows: "The path of thy forefathers leads thy steps to safety and truth." It is also said, "He who follows his own way shall be led astray." If that man's mind was sane, others might have followed him, but there was none who did so, not even his own wife. Thus he was alone in his belief, and it is current among the rest of the nations that the voice of the majority is the voice of truth, insomuch that they say, "The voice of the people is the voice of God."

This is indeed the general impression; for of the large number of learned teachers who are well known for their understanding of the hidden mysteries of the words of the Law, and who have left behind them several books, none did presume what this man has affirmed in his doings. There were, indeed, men who could support their claims with greater logic and in more charming style, but may God forbid that any teacher, whether it be in the days of God's favor or in these days of darkness, should do likewise. This man was led further by his ignorance, so much so that he set apart the day of fasting, from the rest of the festival days, and on it he claimed that no fire should be made. He lied twice in this statement; for he applied to this day a statement which was given particularly for the sake of the Sabbath. But if it applies to this day, why not to the rest of the festival days, which have, on the whole, the same general plan and regulations?

If one should say that, in regard to the past, the Torah has declared *Shebet Shebet*, namely, "A Sabbath to be kept," he could not infer from it that fire should not be made therein; for these same words were mentioned in reference to the year of rest. Compare Leviticus 25:2, "Thou shalt keep a Sabbath unto the land"; and apparently, according to him, fire must not be made during that entire year! But, with all that, work was not prohibited. May God preserve us from doing after the manner of this ignorant heretic, who was trying to establish an ugly heritage. May he protect us from committing a similar error, and inspire us always with obedience to him, and faithfulness to his worship. May he bring us nearer to his pleasure. Verily he is a faithful hearer. May he also bring to guidance this ignorant man, and take him off from his folly; for truly he is in the lowest depth of ignorance. May he examine his condition, and wake up in his soul, and combat himself and let folly alone, and repent of his deed, and return to God, to the supreme and exalted God, with a repentance that is pure and unselfish. If he will do this, God may return to him, for he is merciful and gracious, for thus he spoke of himself to those who may seek him, in Deuteronomy 4:29, "Return to thy God, and he shall not forget thee, nor forget the covenant which he has made with thy forefathers."

End of the Condemnation

Let us now return to what may be said concerning the fulfillment of the Passover ordinance. For our words have been, so far, quite brief in mentioning the conditions of its fulfillment.

There remains yet a condition that the eating of the Passover is obligatory upon every Israelite, whether he be present or absent, and if he be *tameth*, namely, "defiled." The eating of unleavened bread must last seven days completely from sunset of the fourteenth of the first month; that is, from the beginning of the night of the fifteenth till sunset of the twenty-first up till beginning of the night of the twenty-second. In accordance with Exodus 12:17-19, "an eternal ordinance. In the first month on the fourteenth day thereof at sunset ye shall eat unleavened bread until the twenty-first day of the month at sunset. Ye shall eat seven days," namely, seven complete days. This is an eternal ordinance. The fulfillment thereof is obligatory; for it is like circumcision; there is no escape therefrom. But at the beginning of night of the twenty-second day at sunset the end of these seven days is declared without subtraction. And he who eats leavened bread in those seven days must perish in accordance with the command of God in Exodus 12:19, "He who shall eat leavened bread shall be cut off from the people of Israel whether he be a stranger or a native of the land." The destroying of all leavened food in all the dwellings of Israel has been emphasized again and again even in the places where their works, whether the dwelling of man be in a vineyard or in a garden or in a field, even the instruments of plowing and planting, must not be defiled therewith, for thus God said in Deuteronomy 16:4, "And there shall be no leaven seen with thee in all thy borders seven days." Some of our learned men went so far as to prohibit the keeping of *Burgol*, which is wheat boiled and coarsely ground, or even bran, or any kind of leaven. They advise that such be taken before the coming of the feast and be deposited in the houses of neighbors among *Haggoyim* [the Gentiles], and be returned after the passing of the feast, namely, the seven days of unleavened bread. I presume that this advice is due to the extremity to which our people may be reduced in destroying all leaven, for they indulge in those materials which have been mentioned. They (may God multiply them), at the approach of the feast, about the beginning of the first month, begin to clean up all their food receptacles by putting a new coating of white zinc on their brazen dishes and by buying new implements, such as china dishes and ware, glasses, water jars, cups, and water pitchers. They also clean their houses both in the interior and exterior. They wash all they have of carpets, rugs, counterpanes, and blankets, leaving nothing of household implements that may not be washed. All this is done before the arrival of the feast. Still we go in this generation to make our Passover in the plains outside of the town on Mount Gerizim in the tents. We leave for that place two or three days before the feast, and remain there till the second feast, remaining seven days on the mountain until the morning. We do according to the command given in Deuteronomy 16:7-8, namely, "In the morning direct thyself, and return to thy dwellings [tents]. Six days shalt thou eat unleavened food; and on the seventh day there shall be a solemn assembly to the Lord thy God. Thou shalt do no manner of work therein." And thus we do nowadays to the favor of the exalted God. We pass seven days in our tents; and the day of convocation, which is the seventh, we leave our tents for the holy dwelling, which is the place of the temple and altar, and there we perform our duties; and when the convocation has ended, each returns to his tent and attends to his needs. At sunset they gather about the high priest, each having in his hand some *hachamess*, "unleavened bread," and the high priest reads, in company with those present, beginning with the words, "For in the day of Jehovah," and so on to the end of that surah.

After this, the surah beginning with the words "And the blood was," to the end of that surah. They receive three addresses, reciting everything in good order, and then they eat unleavened bread. On the morning of the following" day they immediately descend the mountain, each going to his own business.

We have been brief in our words, avoiding lengthy and tiresome details, but the one who desires to read further concerning the subject may be well satisfied in reading the book called "*Attabakh*," attributed to the learned and wise sheik Hasam Assoory of Tyrus. May God grant him forgiveness and gather us with him in the garden of delight. Amen.

V. THE PASSOVER WHEN THE DATE FALLS ON THE SABBATH

To the question, Suppose that the Passover should fall on the Sabbath, why is it that sacrifices must take place on the day Friday after sunset, and what are the reasons therefore? My answer here follows.

> And my success comes from God.
> Praise be to him who is a generous Giver,
> Who directs to the right path,
> Who does according to his own will,
> And as he chooses to do.

In answer to this question, namely, of offering the sacrifice of the Passover when it falls on the Sabbath, and why we are obliged to kill the sacrifice on Friday, I would say, first, that on the Sabbath all manner of work is absolutely prohibited, in accordance with the words of the Ten Commandments, "Do not do any work on it, for he who does any work on it shall die." References of this nature are many in which work is prohibited on the Sabbath. On this account our learned men (may the Lord grant them forgiveness) inferred that the Passover should be done on Friday, as he said. "Do not leave anything of it until the morning." Then he added, "and whatever may be left of it until the morning ye shall burn with fire"; for this addition is surely meant to be performed in case the Passover falls on the Sabbath, for why should God repeat in the same line the same prohibition given before? He said, also, in another place, in Deuteronomy 16:4, "There shall not be left any of the flesh which thou shalt sacrifice on the first day until the morning." This, also, would indicate to us that the sacrifice would take place only at sunset. It surely explains what must be done in case the Passover falls on the Sabbath. For the sacrifices then may be eaten on the Sabbath; and should there be left any bones or parts of it or flesh, they must all be burned in the night of Sunday. The following reference is given in regard to the sacrifice of the Passover when it happens on the Sabbath: "On the first month on the fourteenth day of the month, between the two evenings, ye shall have the Passover for the Lord" (Leviticus 23:5). Now God did not mention "between the two evenings," except when he had in view the falling of the Passover on the Sabbath. The evenings with us number three: first, the going down of the sun in a westerly direction; second, the immersion of the disk of the sun into the sea; and, third, the disappearance of the redness of the western skies from the sun. Now, whenever the Passover falls on the Sabbath, the killing of the sacrifices takes place as the sun goes down, that is, after six o'clock of the fourteenth. The ordinance of the Sabbath must not be violated; therefore, whatever may be left of the sacrifice is placed under watch until the night of the Sabbath after sunset, and should be burned then on the altar, in the manner that we have already mentioned. And to God belongs the best wisdom.

MOUNT GERIZIM

A few words affirming that Mount Gerizim is the chosen place; and replying to the Jews, who claim that the place was intended to be chosen, and was chosen, only at the hand of Solomon; and convincing all with testimonies taken from the Law, well known and of legal nature, in a brief manner. And to God belongs the best wisdom.

Our opponents claim that the chosen place appears only at the hand of Solomon, and that there was no real temple in Israel before the time of that king. Thus they attribute to the exalted Creator (to whom be praise) but little knowledge of the past and future, for surely he could not have known about the chosen place or he would have indicated it to his chosen, to whom he made great revelations. But God is higher, far above these things, for they are contradicted strongly by passages of the Law. What otherwise did God mean by his command to Abraham (to whom be peace) in Genesis 12:1, "Now move out of thy land, and of the place of thy birth, and of the house of thy father, and into the land which I shall reveal unto thee,"? Then it is said about Abraham: "And Abraham went into the land unto the place of Shechem, unto the plain of Moreh. Then the angels of the Lord appeared to him and announced to him the grant of this land unto his seed," (verse 9). From this same chapter we read: "And the angel of the Lord appeared unto Abraham and said unto him, To thy seed will I give this land." And this took place while our lord Abraham was living in the land of Ur. And when God tried Abraham, asking him to sacrifice his son, our lord Isaac (upon whom be peace), God's command was given in this manner (Genesis 22:2): "Take thy only son, Isaac, whom thou lovest, and go with him, journeying unto the land of Moreh," etc.

Now Abraham obeyed the command of the Lord, and brought his son to the place indicated to him by God; and after his son was redeemed, he said in the same chapter, "God is seen," which is to mean today, "In a mountain God is seen," meaning in a mountain God answers prayers quickly. This is as much as was said about the mountain in the days of our lords Abraham and Isaac (upon whom be peace). Concerning what was said about it in the days of our lord Jacob (upon whom be peace), we may write that when Jacob went to his uncle Laban, he slept in the chosen place and had a dream, in which he saw a ladder reaching the high heavens; and when he arose from his sleep he said: "No doubt this is the house of God and the gate of heaven" (Genesis 28:17). Then he made a vow to God, which was conditional upon God's favor and mercy. Compare Genesis 18:20-22, "And Jacob vowed a vow, saying, If God be with me, and preserve me on this road which I am passing, and if he give me bread to eat, and clothes to wear, and if I return in peace to the house of my father, God will be my master, and this stone, which I have set up as a pillar, shall be the house of God. Also whatever thou giveth to me I shall surely tithe it for thee." And after his return from his uncle's in possession of his desire and fulfillment of his purpose which he prayed from his Lord, it is said in Genesis 33:18, "And Jacob entered the city of Nablous [Shechem] in peace." There he fulfilled what he had vowed upon himself to the exalted Lord. From these testimonies it becomes plain unto us, and we fully realize that the standing of Mount Gerizim is above all others. To it the prayer of Moses refers in his hymn which he sung by the sea as in Exodus 15:17, "Thou shalt bring them, and plant them in the mountain of thy inheritance, in the place which the Lord has chosen for his dwelling, which thy hand has prepared, O God." Then he prayed for the upbuilding of this place, as, in the same verse, we read, "O Lord, build it up by thy might." These passages do affirm unto us that there was then in existence a chosen place, known to our fathers, Abraham, Isaac, and Jacob (upon whom be peace). If, however, we should surrender, and say, as our opponents do, that our lord Abraham went to Jerusalem, and there he offered his son Isaac as a sacrifice; that our lord Isaac slept and dreamed there, and made a vow in the same, why was not Jerusalem singled out and made known as a chosen place? Why was it left for David and Solomon to discover that their great forefathers had been in error in supposing Mount Gerizim to be the real sanctuary? Such a belief is faulty, and cannot be trusted by a sane mind, namely, that our most high and exalted Jehovah would command his prophets to go to places which are unchosen and unknown. God (may his name be praised) is above all such insinuations. The Jews err, and God is infallible. So much is enough for those who desire the truth, and I pray God for his help in avoiding false testimony and fallacious argumentation. Verily he knows the unknown, and covers the sins of those who groan from their iniquities.

VI. THE FORTY YEARS IN THE WILDERNESS

I was asked by some, How long did the children of Israel remain in the wilderness, and were the forty years solar or lunar? Did they offer the Passover sacrifice and eat the unleavened bread, or did they not offer the sacrifice of the Passover and eat unleavened bread, or did they practice circumcision during their stay in the wilderness, as our opponents claim? Did they offer the daily sacrifices or not, and the monthly sacrifices, and those of the feast, while they had with them the Shekinah, and fire was kept continually on the altar?

The children of Israel fulfilled all the ordinances which they were commanded in the Torah, among them the Passover ordinance, for it is one of the greatest ordinances. Our fathers used to perform it according to the rules and regulations, and ate it with unleavened bread and bitter herbs throughout the forty years. Our opponents claim that our fathers ceased from celebrating the Passover during the period of forty years which they spent in the wilderness. Against this statement I appeal to God! How could they attend to this ordinance while they were in Egypt, surrounded by the most oppressive conditions, and then neglect it when they entered the wilderness with perfect liberty, and while Moses (upon whom be peace) was with them? How could they cease from performing an ordinance which was given to them as long as the world lasts, being at the time in a place where no one would oppose them?

CATTLE FOR SACRFICE IN THE WILDERNESS

I am asked, Whence did they obtain the sacrifices, since they were in the wilderness and had no cattle? Nay, they had their cattle with them, and it is the same with which they left Egypt. Compare Exodus 12:38, "Also went with them a mixed multitude, and sheep and oxen and cattle in a large number." Of these they used to offer their daily sacrifices, and whatever sacrifices were required, according to the times and seasons. They, made the unleavened bread from the manna which was daily brought down upon them, and was their food for a period of forty years. If the opponents say that manna cannot be called bread, I will answer that such a name be applied to it, for the Lord did so design it before bringing it down to them: "Behold, I am raining upon you bread from heaven" (Exodus 16:4).

Now as to the period of forty years complete, I would say that the manna was given them during that period, less two months of the first year. And it is said that it did not cease from them except when they encamped in the plain of Moreh, by the side of Mount Gerizim. The verse "They ate the manna until they entered into the boundaries of the land of Canaan" (Exodus 16:35), means that the same ceased from being given to them when they arrived at the boundaries of the land of Canaan. As the verse "The children of Israel ate manna forty years" means the forty years were fulfilled, including the month and a half or two which transpired of the first year without the manna. On the fifteenth day of the forty-first year, when they began to eat of the fruits of the land, the falling of manna ceased. Then they surely must have crossed the Jordan on the tenth of the first month of that year, which, according to tradition, may have been Tuesday, or more accurately Wednesday. They stopped in the Gilgal on Thursday, and they ate manna in it, and on Friday they went out and gathered three omers of manna for each, which, according to our traditions, is due to the fact that the blessed feast of the Passover took place in that period. Some of our best chroniclers say that the Passover took place on Monday. Thus their first feast in the Holy Land was the Passover, and that on Monday, for they ate it of unleavened bread made of the flour of the land which they baked; and this is the true version of it, I think.

Those who claim that those who entered into the wilderness or were born during the forty years were not circumcised make a terrible mistake. What prohibited them from doing so, for they were commanded with this ordinance from the times of our lord Abraham (upon whom be peace). They understood how absolute and definite are the punishments of those who do not perform it. Passages to that effect are numerous, for whosoever is born among the Israelites, and is not circumcised on the eighth day, is not counted with the people, and that soul is destroyed from the number of its people. What our opponents claim in this matter is unacceptable and irrational, and so much is enough in this brief treatise. I pray thee, God, for the attainment of my desire and the grace of avoiding falsehood and error. Amen, O God, and Amen.

VII. THE FASTS OF MOSES

A question concerning the fasting of our lord Moses: Was it forty days during the first fasting, and forty days during the second only, or did he undergo three fastings, namely three forties, according to what our learned men have informed us? May God's pleasure be upon them all.

When did these fastings begin, and when did they end? The answer is given through a plain Scriptural statement. And God possesses the best knowledge.

The fastings of our lord Moses (may peace be his portion) were three in number, each lasting forty days. The first one is mentioned in the surah beginning with *Alah Alai-Haharah*, where, in Exodus 24:18, we read: "And Moses was on the mountain forty days and forty nights." Now when Moses (upon whom be peace) departed from the presence of God, and went down and saw what the people were doing, and beheld that accursed calf, with that frightful scene around it, he threw the two tablets from his hand and broke them at the base of the mountain, doing what we read was done with the worshipers of the calf, for God destroyed them in that time. Thus we read in Exodus 32:30-31, "And in the morning Moses said to the people, Ye have sinned a great sin, and I am about to ascend before God and pray, and perhaps I will intercede for your sins; therefore Moses returned to God." There he fasted for the second time forty days, while interceding for the people, until God had accepted his prayers and had forgiven the people. We know this from Deuteronomy 9:18, "Then I prayed before Jehovah, as before, and during forty days and forty nights I neither ate bread nor drank water, because of your sins which ye have committed to do the evil thing before Jehovah to offend him."

We know, besides, that God commanded him to make two other tablets like the first one and commanded him to engrave them, as it is revealed in Exodus 34:1, "Jehovah said unto Moses, Hew thee two tablets of stone like the two first ones," etc. And in the second line of the same chapter we read: "And be ye ready in the morning, and ascend in the morning unto Mount Sinai." It is well known that this command of God (may his name be praised) was given after the second fasting of forty days. Compare Deuteronomy 10:1, "At that time Jehovah said unto me, Hew thee two tables of stone like unto the first." Moses hewed unto himself the second two stone tablets on that day, and on the following he went with them up into the mountain, for we read in Exodus 34:2, "And be ye ready in the morning, and go up in the morning to Mount Sinai, and stand there before me upon the top of the mountain. Let no man go up with thee."

While on this mountain he fasted forty days for the third time. For we read in the same chapter, namely, Exodus 34:27-28, "And Jehovah said unto Moses, 'Write thou these words for after the tenor of these words I have made a covenant with thee and with Israel.' And he was there with Jehovah forty days and forty nights; he did neither eat bread, nor drink water. And he wrote upon the tables the words of the covenant, the Ten Commandments." It is known, also, from the Torah, that the first fasting of the apostle Moses (may the peace of God be upon him) began on Friday, which is known with us as the day *Kohleh-Ha-Ibrim* ("the gathering of Hebrews"); for on Monday God commanded him in Exodus 19:10-11, "And Jehovah said unto Moses, Go unto the people, and sanctify them today and tomorrow, and let them wash their clothes. And be ready against the third day; for the third day Jehovah will come down in the sight of all the people upon Mount Sinai." The third day would be Wednesday, which is with us the Pentecost day, and on that day the righteous God (may he be praised) uttered the Ten Commandments, which day became with them a great day, whose importance has kept well known until our days. It is named "the Day of *Mekratah*." On that selfsame day Moses pronounced, in the hearing of the people, the Ten Commandments, as stated in Exodus 19:25, "So Moses went down unto the people, and spoke unto them." He gave them an exposition of God's statutes and what God had addressed to him, for we read in Exodus, "Thus shalt thou say to the house of Jacob and announce to the children of Israel"; and we read also: "And Moses came and explained to the people all the commandments of the Lord and all his statutes." He also did what is given in Exodus 24:4, "And Moses wrote all the words of Jehovah, and rose up early in the morning, and built an altar under the hill, and twelve pillars, according to the twelve tribes of Israel." And that morning was the morning of the fifth day, which was Thursday, as mentioned by the learned doctor Sadakah in his exposition book. On that day they offered sacrifices upon the altar, and what Moses has written of the commands of God was read to them.

VIII. THE WRITING OF THE COMMANDMENTS

We have been asked, "What was the use of writing the commandments of God and reading them to the people after the people had been addressed directly with them, and after they had answered, 'All the words which Jehovah hath said will we do' (Exodus 24:3)?"

The answer is like this: A man will agree with another upon some thing. He writes first the agreement and reads it to him. The second party agrees or disagrees to the agreement, and that is why the people answered, "We will do," in Hebrew, *Nesheh*. They said the second time, "We shall obey and do," equivalent to *Nechmoa Unecheh* in the Hebrew. And when the young man of Israel had killed the offerings of oxen upon the altar which the apostle had built, the latter took the blood, and put half of it in basins, and the other half he sprinkled on the altar; but the half which was kept in the basin he sprinkled over the children of Israel. Thus the blood fell upon their clothing and the Ten Commandments *Eshret Hadebarim* were inscribed upon the people according as they were heard from the mouth of the Almighty God, who made a covenant with them, according to Exodus 24:8, "And he said, Behold the blood of the covenant, which Jehovah has made with you concerning all these words." In another place, namely, Exodus 34:27, we read, "According to the tenor of these words I have made a covenant with thee and with Israel." This covenant was made with them, that they might not commit any transgression in the commandments of the High God (whose name is exalted). It is the fourth commandment of the seven which God had made with the children of Israel. And God knows best, and to him belongs the best wisdom.

Now, after the fulfillment of all these things, God said, in Exodus 24:12, "Elah, Elai Haharah," namely, "Come up to me to the mountain." This, therefore, according to the revelation, was on Friday, upon which his first fastings took place. On the morning of the forty-first day he descended the mountain, and found what the people had done in reference to the calf, and took the same, and burned it on that very day. It is well known what he did on that day. On the following morning he returned to the mountain to intercede for the people and for their transgressions, as we have already stated. He remained there fasting for forty days, and on the fulfillment of the forty days he descended, and hewed out the two tablets on the day of his descent. On the morning he returned and ascended the mountain, to obtain the writing upon the second two tablets. Compare Exodus 34:2, "And be ready by the morning, and come up by the morning unto Mount Sinai." Thus the whole period previous to this amounted to eighty-two days. After he had fasted another forty days, the period totaled one hundred and twenty-two days plus the day on which he descended. Now, as four days had proceeded, namely, Monday, Tuesday, Wednesday, and Thursday, and as doubtless one day or two were omitted from one month, the descent of the apostle Moses (upon whom may be the best peace), after the end of the third forty days, was, in all probability, on the morning of the ninth day of the seventh month, that is, on the day known with us as *Teshet Iomey Hateshobah*, that is, "the nine days of repentance."

On that day Moses commanded the people to fast on the tenth of the seventh month, known with them as "the day of the great atonement," in Hebrew *Iom Hakeforim*. This is in accordance with what our learned doctor of blessed memory, Sadakah, has said.

This account would be true if the third month had fallen on Monday. If it had fallen on the Sabbath, then the omission of only one day in the four months we have mentioned could have taken place, for it is impossible that four months should occur without the omission of a single day, as our learned men claim that the new moon of the first month in which the Passover was celebrated in Egypt took place on Thursday. This is quite proved. Thus, following in the least these accounts, we would think that one month in these six months had been omitted; and it is said that the six days which are mentioned in Exodus 24:16, "And a cloud covered it for six days," were included in the fasting of the apostle Moses in his first fasting. And God has the best knowledge of all these things.

This is what my tired understanding and weak mind have been able to record concerning this question, and I pray God for forgiveness if any addition or subtraction has been made.

IX. THE REVELATION OF THE TORAH

I have been asked by some concerning the noble Torah, as to the time of its revelation, and whether it was revealed all at once, or at different times according to the events. What Biblical explanations could be given which are of a convincing nature?

Let it be known unto thee, O questioner, that the holy Torah was revealed in one roll by the supreme righteous God, written in the handwriting of the Almighty, in characters that are well known, containing all the verses and divisions and commands and prohibitions and explanations and other knowledge from the very beginning to the end. This is according to what our most learned high priest Hasam Assoory of Tyrus has written in his book, known as the book of "Tabach." They err, those among our people (whom may God diminish) claiming that the commandments of the Torah and its prohibitions were addressed to the apostle Moses (upon whom be peace), who wrote them down himself. Now their claim is wrong, from various points of view.

Take, for instance, the question of the manna. It was given to the people on the sixteenth day of the second month of the first year of their departure from Egypt, and continued to be given unto them while they were in the wilderness for a period of forty years, both solar and lunar, until they arrived in the land of Canaan. Compare Exodus 16:35, "And the children of Israel ate the manna for forty years, until they arrived in an inhabited land. They ate the manna until they arrived at the borders of Canaan." Consider, for instance, the question of sprinkling the water which he commanded to be done in the ninth day of the first month of the second year of their departure from Egypt. Examples of this nature can be multiplied. Thus it is plain that the apostle Moses (upon whom be peace) received delivered unto him all the Torah written in all perfection. Of this there are various proofs.

First, God does not create anything unless he provides for its necessity and usefulness. To verify my statement concerning the Torah, I will begin citing Exodus 24:12, "Ascend unto me to the mountain, and be there: and I will give thee the two tablets, and the law and the commandments, which I have written down for their instruction." The words "the law" and "the commandments" refer to the roll of the Law, which is the Torah, without the least doubt. We can prove that this one referred to is found in the same book, chapter 32:32, "Otherwise blot me out from thy roll which thou hast written." The word *Sepher* means "roll" wherever it is found, although some interpreters render it by the word "book."

Second, that the Torah was revealed and came down completely in one roll is proved by the fact that it mentions events before their happening. Compare, for instance, what God has said concerning the river which comes out of the garden and which divides into four parts. The first part surrounds the land of "Hewilah," which is Egypt. The second surrounds the land of the Soudan. The third is that which runs east of the land of Mosul. The fourth is the Euphrates. This statement was given in the beginning of creation, before the existence of either Egypt or

Soudan or any other country. Then when God created Eve out of the rib of our father Adam (upon whom be peace), he said in Genesis 24:29, "Therefore shall a man leave his father and mother, and cleave unto his wife." Then there were neither father nor mother and none but Adam and Eve, and this was the first commandment given unto the seed of Adam.

Third, what was meant by the reference to the age of Moses, the son of Amram, in Genesis, "And his days shall be one hundred and twenty years"?

Fourth, the statement concerning the daughters of Lot, wherein it was said about the first, "And the oldest gave birth to a son whom she called Moab, and he is the father of Moab unto this day"; and of the second, "And the younger gave birth to a son whom she called Ben-Ammi, and he is the father of the children of Ammon unto this day" (Genesis 19:37-38). Now the saying "unto this day" is to mean that the same could be applied to the end of generations.

Fifth, the report of God of the death of our lord Isaac (upon whom be peace) which should have been given after the story of our lord Joseph (upon whom be peace), for the death of Isaac took place after Joseph had passed twelve years in Egypt.

Sixth, we can find proof in Genesis 36:31 where it is said: "These are the kings which reigned in Edom, before there reigned a king of the children of Israel." The names of the kings are there given, and the last king was Hadad. He was the same king concerning whom verse 14 of chapter 20 of Numbers is given: "And Moses sent messengers from Kadesh to the king of Edom," who was really Hadad, in accordance with the instructions of our learned men. For in Leviticus 36 all the kings were said to have died, with the exception of the last one, whose death was not mentioned, and who did not die until after the children of Israel had possessed the land. Besides, everything that was mentioned in the first book, which was Genesis, took place before the time of our lord Moses (upon whom be peace).

Seventh, the question of manna is another proof. It was sent down on the sixteenth day of the second month. The statement which reads, "And the children of Israel ate the manna to the end," was given at the beginning of the fortieth year; and if the Torah had not descended upon Moses in one single year, this statement would not have been written down at the end of the fortieth year.

Eighth, God said that there should be a place of refuge for a man who has killed another man unknowingly, and that the refugee should remain in the place until the death of the high priest. Now this statement was written at the end of the fourth book, and these places were to be established after the conquest of the holy land. We find it, however, mentioned in the second book, which is Exodus, in the surah beginning with chapter 21, verse 7. Read, therefore, verse 13, "Make therefore a place of refuge for him, that he may flee thereto." This statement was given at the beginning of the fortieth year, but the children of Israel had no high priest, nor had they the order of the priesthood. Similar examples might be cited to prove our point.

Now, as to those who claim that the Torah was given piece by piece in accordance with the events that happened, then it must have descended on several prophets, beginning with our lord Adam, the father of all mankind (upon whom be peace), and ending with the last, who is Joshua; for the Torah closes with Moses (may peace be his portion), and the installment of Joshua, his successor (upon whom be peace). Now, if any one should say, "Every prophet wrote the happenings of his days during his lifetime, and the same was done by our lord Moses, who wrote everything in the Law," this supposition is liable to faults and exaggerations, and Moses could not help writing down every statement of the least portion of the contents of the Torah. Supposing that this is true, who, then, wrote down the account of the creation and the things that took place before the life of our father Adam, and who wrote the account of the tower of Babel and what happened to its builders? Surely they did not do it!

Who wrote the affair of the daughters of Lot? For their father knew nothing of it, as we read in Genesis 19:33-35, proving his entire innocence. Surely it could not be true that the daughters themselves reported it! And who might have informed us of the affair of Tamar, the daughter-in-law of Judah? She surely would not have reported the truth. And then, again, during the life of Moses, who was present with Balak and Balaam, who may be considered worthy of belief, that he might inform Moses of the same, that the latter might write it down as the Torah gives it in detail, and also concerning the ass of Balaam and the language which he spoke? God indeed understands all languages. He knows what is visible and invisible. I suppose the speech of the ass was in the same speech which Balaam understood, and God used a language which was understood by the people of that land, namely, Hebrew.

We know, also, that the Torah was given in one single roll by reading and understanding its contents; for, if it had been given in accordance with the progress of the events as they happened, it would have been written in the style of a history. But the style is indeed quite different. The visit of Jethro to his brother-in-law, that is, to Moses, was mentioned, as well as the advice he gave to our lord Moses (upon whom be peace) in Exodus 18. The account concludes with verse 27, "And Moses sent his father-in-law, and he went to his land;" but the exact date of the departure of Jethro is given in Numbers, just on the day the people of Israel left Mount Sinai. Chapter 10, verse 29 says: "And Moses said to Hobab, the son of Raguel, the father-in-law of Moses (for Jethro was called also Hobab), We are about to leave."

In Exodus the erecting of the tabernacle on the first day of the first month of the second year of the departure of the children of Israel from Egypt was mentioned (read Exodus 16:33). From these we know that the tabernacle was erected and finished on the first month of the second year, and on the first day of the month. We know also, that whenever the cloud disappeared from over the tabernacle, the children of Israel would move onward, and this was the uniform beginning of their journeys. So much only is said, but what has been said is again affirmed in Leviticus 1:1, "And Jehovah called out Moses, and spoke to him out of the tabernacle of the congregation, saying," etc. But after the end of the third book and whatever it contained of meanings and advice, Numbers - which is the fourth book, takes up the same question again. It begins: "And Jehovah spake unto Moses in the wilderness of Sinai, in the tabernacle of the congregation, on the first day of the second month of the second year after their departure from the land of Egypt, saying, Count up the congregation of the children of Israel," etc., which is plain enough. Therefore, it must be understood that one month after the erection of the tabernacle, God commanded that the children of Israel be numbered, that the census be taken of the tribes of the children of Israel. But nearly one fourth of the book may be read before the question of the completion of the erection of the tabernacle is taken up, in chapter 7 in the first verse, which reads: "And it came to pass on the day when Moses had fully set up the tabernacle, and had anointed it and sanctified it," etc. Now if the events should have been consecutively mentioned in accordance with their time order, this surah and all that follows it as far as chapter 9, verse 15, which reads: "And in the day of the erection of the tabernacle," etc., should either begin the book of Leviticus or be an end to the book of Exodus.

Also the surah beginning with Numbers 6:22, which reads: "And Jehovah spake unto Moses, saying, Speak unto Aaron and unto his sons, saying, In this way ye shall bless the children of Israel, saying unto them, Jehovah bless thee, and keep thee," etc., should have come before the surah mentioned in Leviticus 9:22, which reads: "Then Aaron lifted up his hand towards the people, and blessed them," etc. The command of the blessing is given in Numbers 6:22, while the fulfillment of it is previously mentioned in Leviticus 9:22. While the blessing takes place, the water of consecration should be sprinkled over the people, which was the part of Mishael and Elzaphan when they picked up Nadab and Abihu, the sons of Aaron, and moved them when they were dead. Thus they were defiled with the defilement of the dead person. Therefore God commanded that this water of consecration be instituted on their account. This was on the eighth day of consecration, but the preparation of the water of consecration took place on the ninth day of the first month of the second year of their departure from the land of Egypt, but the purification of Elzaphan and Mishael must have taken place only on the night of the fifteenth day of the month, which is the night of the Passover, and they could not perform the Passover nor eat it on account of the pollution, therefore God commanded the doing of the second Passover on their account. To prove this we will state that ever since God commanded that the Passover should be performed on the night of the fifteenth of the first month of the second year, this has been so done. So he made plain statements in regard to the second Passover, in Numbers 9:6 and the following verses, during that year to be performed for the benefit of the polluted man, which, according to our learned doctor, were the abovementioned men. This is a remarkable example of mentioning events without regard to their chronological order. Examples of this nature are many, and we do not intend to mention them, for we believe if the apostle Moses (upon whom be peace) had written down the events as they transpired, a due attention would have been given to chronological order.

Concerning Specific Records Made by Moses

If one should ask, "How could you explain Exodus 12:14?", the answer is, God commanded Moses (upon whom be peace) to write the memorial of the blotting out of the Amalekites, and read the same to Joshua (upon whom be peace), to acquaint him with it, although the learned high priest Sadakah, of blessed memory, wrote in regard to this roll, which is mentioned in the aforesaid verse, that Moses had it to remind him of events which he would copy into the Torah when later he compiled the complete work. This statement of the high priest will be refuted later on. Now the meaning of this verse is the same as that found in Exodus 24:4, namely, "And Moses wrote down all the words of God"; and verse 7 reads: "And Moses took the roll of the covenant, and read it in the hearing of the people." In the same manner we read Numbers 5:23.

The Cases where Moses was in Uncertainty concerning the Divine Will

Now if one should say, granting that the apostle Moses (upon whom be peace) received the whole Torah, containing all the events, why is it that in Leviticus 24:12 we find Moses somewhat undecided as to the case of the son of Shelomith when he blasphemed the name of Jehovah, namely, that Moses put this man in prison until Jehovah should reveal unto them his will? Again, in 9:7 when he was asked, "Why should we cease from offering to God the sacrifices in their season?" He answered in the following verse, "Wait until I hear what Jehovah shall command unto you." Again, when they found a man cutting wood on the Sabbath, and brought him before the apostle Moses, he said in Numbers 15:34, "Let him be kept under guard until it may be known what must be done with him." And nothing was done until an answer was returned, as the holy Torah asserts.

When the apostle Moses (upon whom be peace) received the roll, he placed it in his tent, as it is mentioned in Exodus 33:7, "And Moses removed the tent, and erected it outside of the encampment, far from the encampment, and called it the meeting tent." In the beginning of the month he received a command from God to read the Torah, and to write a copy of it as it is written in Deuteronomy 1:3, "In the fortieth year, in the eleventh month, on the first day of the month," etc. And then verse 5, "Moses had begun to copy this law." He used to be the judge of Israel during those forty years, as we read in Exodus 18:16, "I judge between man and man, and acquaint them with the commandments of God and his laws." Whenever he met with difficulties he used to have recourse to God for enlightenment, lest false judgments might be rendered - for he was far above false judgments. As to the time when he received the roll, according to the most learned man, the relative of ours, the one of blessed memory, Hasam Assoory of Tyrus, in his book called "Attabakh," the roll was given to Moses at the end of his forty days' fast, when he received the two tablets which were later dashed to pieces. My opinion, and I pray God for forgiveness if I am mistaken, is that Moses received it at the end of "his second forty days' fast"; for in his first fast he received the first two tablets; and during his second fast he received the roll of the law; and during his third forty days' fast he received the second two tablets. This conclusion may be reached from the wording of the law. And God possesses the best knowledge.

It was for this roll that our lord Moses removed his tent outside of the encampment, and placed in it the roll, the tent being called the "meeting tent." Our lord Joshua was its guard, keeping it in this tent in accordance with Exodus 33:2, where we read: "And his servant Joshua Ben Nun did not go out of the middle of the tent." Do you not see that the apostle took him in his company during the first forty days' fast, as we read in Exodus 24:13, "And Moses and his servant Joshua arose and ascended to the mountain of God," etc.? During the second forty days, Joshua remained at the base of the mountain, gathering his food of the manna, until the descent of Moses with the two tables. What proves that Joshua remained throughout all those days at the foot of the mountain is found in Exodus 32:17; for, when the apostle Moses descended with the two tablets after his fast of forty days, we read: "And Joshua heard the voice of the people in shouting, and he said to Moses, There must be a war cry in the encampment." If he had been present among the people he would not have said this in an inquiring manner.

During the second forty days' fast Joshua did not accompany Moses, nor did anybody else; for we read in Exodus 34:3, "Let no man go up with thee."

If anyone should ask why the high priest Merkah, of blessed memory, said in reference to the decalogue, "And he wrote of them five writings," the meaning is, that the decalogue includes in its explanation the whole Torah. And he who desires to investigate further may look up the commentary of the law written by Aben Hajar, and that of the high priest Merkah, which possess full explanations as to the meaning of the various readings of the law. He declares likewise that the Torah descended as a whole from before the presence of God, written by the very hand of the Almighty, and handed down to his apostle our lord Moses son of Amram (upon whom may be the best of regard). Therefore, as can be seen from several passages chosen from his writings, and from the writings of our crowned poet, our lord Moses son of Amram received the Torah in one roll containing all the ordinances, commandments, and prohibitions, all the news and teachings, which are attributed to have come from God, and which therefore are true and righteous, not liable to addition or detraction, with plain characters inscribed in the very material of the roll with the color of fire, as we read in Deuteronomy, "From his right hand they have a fire of law. Blessed art thou, O Israel. Blessed art thou, for what thy Jehovah has granted to thee, for the high station to which he has raised thee, for the abundance of favors which he has bestowed on thee above all others. Thou art the noble race; from thee the world becomes acquainted with virtue and knowledge; from thee the wise men receive their wisdom, and their laws are derived from thy laws; from its sea of abundance they have drunk; upon it they have relied and to its wisdom they have helped themselves, becoming thereby thy disciples."

Compare Deuteronomy 33:3, "They shall bow before thy feet, and receive instruction from thy words"; for thy ennobling and thy honor that God spoke in Deuteronomy 4:6, "Since thy wisdom and prudence is before the eyes of the Gentiles who will hear all these commands, they will say, Verily this people is wise and prudent and far-seeing." Continue to read to verse 8: "And what people is so great that it has commands and ordinances so just as those found in this law?" Again, verses 32-33: "Ask now of the days that are past, which were before thee, since the day when God created man on earth, and from one end of the heaven to the other end of heaven, whether anything has ever been as this great thing, or whether there has ever been heard anything like it? Did any people ever hear the voice of God speaking out of the midst of fire as thou hast heard, and remain alive?"

Many similar examples could be multiplied which would make the exposition in this book somewhat lengthy. May God make you and us among those who cover us with the cover of righteousness, who put on the cover of righteousness and clothe themselves with the robe of purity. We have taken the privilege to explain fully in regard to this matter, that the obstinate may be made wise and abandon his way. He is ignorant who belies us by saying that the law did not come down from the righteous presence of God in one roll from beginning to end. He ignores the words of God and the meaning of His law. It may suffice us to say that even our opponents, such as *Haggoyim*, testify that no other book came as a whole from before the presence of God except the holy Torah. So much is enough to him who is not swayed by his lust, who follows truth and receives the divine guidance. The Most High God is most righteous, and possesses the best knowledge. I pray his forgiveness for all addition and subtraction.

X. THE TWO STONE TABLETS

I have been asked by some, concerning the two stone tablets which were broken, When were they prepared, and what happened to the writing after the breaking of the tablets? When were the two second tablets placed in the chest? What was their size? What Scriptural grounds can be adduced to prove the answers?

The first two tablets were created by God in the beginning, and some claim that this was done on the third day of the creation, according to the high priest Micah. Others say that the two tablets were prepared when they were needed. We believe that the first statement is more valid. The writing was engraved upon them like the engraving of a signet ring, and was done by the hand of the Almighty. (Compare Exodus 31:18, "written by the fingers of God.") It is said that the two tablets were the creation of God, and that their writings were the writings of the Divine Essence, engraved upon the two tablets which were handed to the apostle Moses by the chief of the angels, that is by Gabriel, the Archangel, at the close of Moses' forty days' fast. Some say that

Moses found them before him at his feet at the place wherein he was tenting while on the mountain. This statement, I believe, (and I pray God to shield me from mistakes,) is more correct than that the Power Divine handed them to him without his seeing anything; for he was standing in darkness listening to the address of God coming from the midst of the fire. The writing was plain on either side, and all the characters were horizontal in shape, without being connected the one with the other. Each tablet was a cubit and a half in length and in breadth, but three fourths of a cubit in height. They fitted the chest wonderfully. The thickness of both of them combined equaled two cubits and a half, in accordance with the height of the chest.

When Moses descended from the mountain and arrived at the outskirts of the encampment, he saw the calf and the frolic scene around it (and may such a scene never take place again), and his anger was boundless, and he dashed the two tablets to the earth in their presence and broke them. But, before doing so, he showed the people the two tablets, their bright likeness and wonderful engraving, declaring to them that God was angry at their deed, and hence they were unfit to receive the tablets. At that moment, God (may his name be exalted) caused the writing to disappear, and commanded Moses (upon whom be peace) to dash them on the ground. If God had not blotted out his writing from the two tablets, it would not have been lawful or possible unto Moses to break them. Thus the same disappeared up to heaven by the power of God, and nobody knew what became of them.

After his second fasting, while he was interceding for this great sin, his prayers having been answered, God commanded him to hew unto himself two tablets like unto the first, having the same shape and size, and to prepare the chest in accordance with their size. He, therefore, following the instruction of God, ascended the mountain and fasted forty days for the third time. And the two tablets were taken away from him and engraved by the hand of God, like the first two, with the Ten Commandments, only without addition or subtraction.

He came down with them on the ninth day of the seventh month, as we have stated already, and placed them in the chest which he had purposely prepared for them in his tent. And he placed them beside the holy Torah until the tabernacle was erected, when he deposited them in that, which Bezaleel had made, as we read in Exodus, "And he took and placed the testimonies in the chest." But the command was given first in Numbers, "And place the testimonies which I give thee in the chest." This was confirmed later on in Numbers: "And it was there as Jehovah commanded." And God possesses the best wisdom.

XI. THE TABLETS OF TESTIMONY

Why were the two tablets called the tablets of testimony and the tablets of stone? They were called the tablets of testimony that they might be a living testimony, written in the correct and original Hebrew language, and containing all the decalogue, against whomsoever may transgress them or change them or garble them. They were called so also, probably, because the children of Israel testified unto themselves to accept them and to act in accordance with all of what God spoke in Mount Sinai in their hearing and presence. Compare Exodus: "Whatever God commanded us we will obey and do." And that is probably why they were called tablets of stone to indicate that they were solid and of hard nature. The meaning, however, is deep, and God only fathoms its secrets.

XII. THE TRANSCRIPTION OF THE TORAH

When was the roll of the law read which was given to our lord Moses son of Amram, when was it transcribed by his noble hand, and when did the children of Israel read the same and learn it, after the death of the apostle?

When the apostle received from God the holy roll, he placed it in his tent outside of the encampment, and God used to speak to him after the fog had encompassed the tent and covered the place where the holy roll was deposited. This was done there when consultation concerning the daily affairs of the people was needed. The commandments, however, were given to him in the tabernacle, between the two cherubim. The roll remained in its place for forty years. It was placed by the side of the chest which Bezaleel had prepared for the two tablets as soon as the tabernacle was erected, as we have stated before. During the first of the eleventh month of the fortieth year, Moses began to copy the holy law, and deposited two copies which he finished in the first month, one with the Levites, the other with the elders. Compare Deuteronomy 31:9, "And Moses wrote this law, and handed it to the priests, the sons of Levi, and to all the elders of Israel." And he taught them its content, as we find in the same chapter, verse 19. Some say that the verse refers to the hymn, as in the verse we read: "And now write for yourself this hymn." But we believe that the meaning refers to all the content of the law; for, at the end of these words, we read: "And after Moses finished writing down the commandments of this law in the roll," etc., he commanded the Levites to take the roll that came from God, and place it beside the chest of the two tablets. Compare Deuteronomy 31:26, "Take the roll of the Torah, and place it by the side of the chest of the covenant of your God, and let it be unto thee a witness."

The death of our lord Moses took place in the beginning of the twelfth month of the fortieth year, and the children of Israel mourned him during that whole month. And on the first day of the first month they left Arabat Moab, and on the tenth of the same they crossed the Jordan.

It is said they crossed the sea on Wednesday, and heard the voice of God on Wednesday, and crossed the Jordan on Wednesday. And unto God belongs all wisdom and power.

XIII. THE JORDAN

If anyone should ask, "What is the Jordan?" Answer: It is the river of the Torah.

They celebrated the Passover after they crossed the Jordan, and on the second day of the feast of the Passover manna disappeared, and they ate from the products of the land and made therefrom unleavened bread. Then they began their seven years' war against the enemy, and on the seventh month of the seventh year they conquered their enemies entirely, and were rested, and erected the tabernacle on Mount Gerizim, which is the chosen place of the dwelling of the Most High God. They built the stone altar in accordance with the command of God, and offered due sacrifice, and fasted during the great day of sin covering, and celebrated the Feast of Tabernacles. On that day the high priest Eleazar son of Aaron began to read the law to the people from the copy handed to them by Moses, the apostle of God, written by his noble hand, as we see in Deuteronomy 15:1, "At the end of seven years," in the first year of rest, when the children of Israel shall celebrate the feast and appear before the Lord thy God in the place which he chose, shalt thou read before them this Torah in the hearing of the children of Israel. He began its reading on the feast day, and on the seventh day it was finished. It is said that he used to read to them some book each day.

He would stand on a high place and would raise his voice so the whole people could hear his words and understand the meaning, and the import of the Torah, what was to them pure and what was impure, the verses that were intended for men and those that were intended for women, all that God commanded that they should do and perform. Compare Numbers 31:12, "Gather ye the people, men and women, and the children and the neighbors and the strangers," that they may hear and be instructed. Some learned men say that, on account of the large number of people and the large space occupied by their tents, the high priest could not make himself understood to the farthest as well as the nearest to him, and therefore he used to adopt two plans: either to gather them in separate numbers and read to each; or to read to the chiefs of the people, the men of understanding, and have them instruct the rest. And God knows best.

It is said that whenever seven years would pass, when the year of rest would take place, the high priest used to enter the tabernacle on the day of Sin Covering to burn incense. He would return, and with him he would have the roll of the Torah, and would read it to the people of Israel, according to one of the above plans during one of the seven days of the Feast of Tabernacles. He would keep the roll throughout that whole year, for the people used to be scattered after their plowing and planting, tree pruning, and the rest of their work. The scribes would present themselves before the high priest and examine the writing of the roll, the placement of characters, and the true spelling. During the second year, on the day of Sin Covering, he would return the roll to its place. Some learned men, however, say that the roll was never removed from its place in the tabernacle. It was only the roll that was written by the hand of Moses that was taken out and shown to the people, which is quite correct. And God knows best the truth.

XIV. THE SHINING OF MOSES' FACE

I was asked by some, concerning the face of our lord Moses son of Amram when it was bright and shone with light, "When did it happen, and how did he use to deal with the people when he used to read to them the words of God?" After the three forty days' fastings, light darted out from him with dazzling effulgence, outwardly and inwardly, and his noble face shone. This was one of the greatest wonders that he performed; for the one who keeps up fasting becomes feeble, he loses his strength, and the energy upon his face is lost. It was the contrary in his case; for, in spite of the long fasting, he shone with a divine light, through the favor of God. This is implied in the saying of God in Exodus 34:10, "With thee I will do wonders again, which have never before been performed in all the earth, and before all men, and in all nations," meaning that none of the jewels of the earth will ever compare in brightness with this light with which he shone. He added, "and in all nations," meaning that there has never been any man among all the peoples of the earth who had ever come near possessing the same.

Verse 11 reads: "And all the people of which thou art will see that the work which the Lord thy God will do thee is wonderful," meaning that this wonder will be seen by the people without their being conscious of it. For we read in Exodus 34:39, "And Moses knew not that the skin of his face began to shine while he was speaking with him." And when he descended from the mountain, the children of Israel, with his brother Aaron, saw him while his face was brighter than the light of the sun. And they were dazzled with his look, and were afraid to approach him, as we read in verse 30, "they were afraid to approach him," although he knew nothing about the condition of his face, for he was like other men, and unable to see his own face. Calling them to draw near, he was informed of what they saw. Therefore he made for himself a face veil, in order that the people might behold him (may the peace of God be upon him). So then, whenever he addressed them, he would uncover his face, and would speak with them the words of God; and when he was through his address they would not be able to behold him. Whenever he went into the presence of God he unveiled himself, but when he addressed the people he put on the veil. And God knows best.

I was asked by some, concerning Exodus 24:10, "And they saw the God of Israel, and there was under his feet as it were a paved work of sapphire stone, as clear as the cloudless heaven. What did they see? They saw indeed our lord Gabriel the Archangel, the servant of the glorious God. To interpret the word *Elohim* as God would be gross ignorance, for God has neither member nor claw, because in the same verse we read: "under his feet." For God (who is exalted) is not seen, and cannot be likened to anything. Compare Exodus 33:20, "For no man shall see me and live."

The word *Elohim* has different interpretations. It may be applied just as the words *Rabbi* and *Adonai* to several titled persons, such as the governor, sultan, etc., the number of which may render this treatise long. Therefore what they saw was not God, but Gabriel, as we have said. He was standing on a platform in the guise of a column as pure as a jewel, and very transparent, as we read in 34:10, "having the transparency of heaven in clearness," that is, as clear as the heaven when it is cloudless. Our lord Gabriel was in the service of *Hakkabod* (Glory), whose look was like the very consuming fire. Compare Exodus 24:17, "And the appearance of the glory of God was like "the very consuming fire on the top of the mountain in the presence of the children of Israel."

At this time they were commanded what we read in Exodus 24:1, "And he said to Moses, Come up thou, and Aaron, and Nadab, and Abihu, and seventy of the elders of Israel, and worship from afar." It is said also, Let Moses and Aaron and Nadab and Abihu and Ithamar come. And they saw the Lord of Israel while they were at the base of the mountain, but the people observed the light from the encampment, as we read in the same chapter, "in the presence of the children of Israel." This was on a different day from that of the day of the address before the decalogue, for there we read in Exodus 19:21, "Hurry down and warn this people, lest they be emboldened to see Jehovah." He also warned him to declare unto the people, even unto the priests, not to approach the mountain. He commanded them to consecrate themselves lest the chief angel should strike them. Compare verse 22: "And let the priests also, that come near unto Jehovah, sanctify themselves, lest the angel of Jehovah strike them down"; and that is why we read in 29:11, "And upon the nobles of the children of Israel he laid not his hand," which means that they, with the exception of the apostles, did not embolden themselves, and did not approach without receiving a command, and did not commit any evil thing without being struck by the Lord. But they were favored with strength and power from on high, when they saw the chief archangel in that wonderful sea.

They returned safely and with gladness, eating and drinking. Compare Exodus 24:11, "And they saw the angel of the Lord, and they ate and drank." Moses, however, did not receive the address which was all made in the presence of the people of Israel.

And I pray God for forgiveness for any addition or subtraction. This is what my tired mind and sickly understanding could discover. And God possesses the best knowledge.

XV. THE WATER AT REPHIDIM

To the question, "What happened in Rephidim of miracles, on account of the lack of water, and its appearance through Moses?" My answer here follows.

Before the war with the Amalekites they encamped in Rephidim and were very thirsty, as when they encamped there, they found no water. They quarreled with the apostle Moses (upon whom be peace), and told him: "Arise, and give us water, that we may drink, together with our children and babes and cattle." But the apostle told them: "Why quarrel ye with me, and tempt Jehovah?" They let him alone; but, on account of their parching thirst, they returned unto him, and said: "Did you intend to bring us out of Egypt that we might perish of thirst? If we ourselves were guilty, and did not deserve to be given water, the children and the cattle, in what have they sinned, that they should die of thirst?" The apostle, knowing that they were to strike him down, cried to God for help, and the answer was immediate: "Pass before the people, and be not afraid, and take with thee some of the elders of Israel."

This was done that they might behold the wonder, and not in company with the people; for the place from which he caused the water to gush forth was far away, and all the people could not behold it. And Jehovah knew that there was no good in their coming to it to behold it. The place was Horeb. In verse 6 it reads, "Behold, I," meaning that the angel will stand in a pillar of cloud in the place which he was to strike.

Arriving, the apostle, in company with the elders, smote the rock with his well-known staff; and behold, the water in abundance flowing out of it, which formed a large river. This river is the one alluded to in Deuteronomy 9:21, "I have cast its dust in the river which flowed from the mountain." It divided into two branches, one branch toward Rephidim and the other toward the wilderness of Sinai, of which they drank during their stay in the wilderness. That place was called *Meribah* in Exodus 17:7, "And he called the name of the place *Massah Meribah*." The first word, *Massah*, refers to their tempting God, as we read in 22:2; and this was due to their great ignorance, lack of faith and trust in the presence of God, and in his power to overcome their hunger and their thirst. Verse 7 proves this; for in it we are told that they said: "Is God among us, or not?" This was prohibited by God, as we read in Deuteronomy 6:16, "Ye shall not tempt Jehovah your God, as ye tempted him in *Massah*." The word "*Meribah*" refers to the quarrel which they had with the apostle. But God knows best.

XVI. THE BATTLE WITH THE AMALEKITES

As to the question of the Amalekites' battle and the reason why the Amalekites came from a far country to fight them in that place, we may answer, that this took place for several reasons. First, that God might remind them of what they had committed in past sins, when they desired water and tempted him, quarreling with his apostle, that they might reform and repent. Second, when the king of the Amalekites heard of the arrival of the children of Israel, and feared lest they would attack his land on account of his courage and his strength of character and his God-offending pride, he sought to fight them in that place, thinking that he would overpower them in the wilderness easier than it would be possible for him had they been in a nearby settled country, thereby showing to the rest of the nations his audacity and boldness. Therefore God sentenced him to perdition, as we read in Numbers 21:20, "The first of the nations is Amalek, but its end is perdition."

XVII. THE REASON FOR NOT DESTROYING THE AMALEKITES EARLIER

Should one ask, "Why did God not destroy, as he was able, the Amalekites before they fought the children of Israel?" We answer, God was surely able to do so, but he allowed this to help him, that it might be an example and a reminder, like the affair of Pharaoh, together with the miracles that took place to his disadvantage and to that of his people; that the children of Israel might know the great favor of God in destroying this Amalek, who was a giant, and greater than he God had never before created; and that they might know the art of war and tactics and courage, so that when Sihon, Og, and the rest should come against them, they would fight without fear.

Again, the coming of this great giant with his Amalekites was for the purpose of destroying all those who complained and quarreled with our lord Moses in connection with the waters. Compare 17:11. As to the real battle, Moses gave its conduct to Joshua son of Nun because he was sure of his courage, and that the apostle Moses might stay on the mountain interceding and praying for success. Of this our lord Moses had informed his disciple Joshua, saying to him, that what he would do would take place on the morrow. At that time, therefore, he ascended the mountain in company with Aaron and Hur - who was the grandfather of Bezaleel who built the tabernacle.

One stood on his right and the other at his left, while the apostle stood interceding and praying, with his hands raised towards heaven towards the holy place, and his staff in his hand. Verse 12 tells us that his hands became tired; and therefore Aaron and Hur supported them, for he was higher than they, as they placed under him a stone, and he sat on it: "But Moses' hands were heavy; and they took a stone, and put under him, and he sat thereon."

Now if some ask, Why did the apostle not keep his hands raised, since he knew that in raising them Israel had victory, and in lowering them Amalek had it? Why did he not keep his hands raised until all the Amalekites had perished? The answer is that this was done in accordance with the command of God when he ordered that others should lower them, that beholders may know the high station he had before God. They, no less than the whole nation, had need to know. This took place, according to what we have kept in our memory, on Friday.

The Standing of the Sun

The battle did not cease at the end of the day. Therefore the sun stopped for a sufficient time to allow Joshua a complete victory over the Amalekites before sunset. Amalek and the people who followed him must be killed before the coming in of the Sabbath, for at the sunset the Sabbath would begin, and Israel would be bound in with its conditions, and could not continue the fight. This we have taken from the book attributed to him and known as the book of Joshua (The Samaritan Book of Joshua). And God knows all these things best.

However, we could infer this from Exodus 17:12, for we read: "And his hands were kept steady until the going down of the sun." This was due, probably, to what we know of the same verse and the preceding one. When Amalek and his people were destroyed, God commanded Moses to write down the record of this battle in a roll, and to read it in the hearing of Joshua, that he and the people might know that God had blotted out the name and the mention of the Amalekites from under the entire heaven, that the people might recover their courage, as they had been terribly afraid, since the giant had come from a very far place to fight them boldly. Then the apostle built in that place an altar, and sacrificed thank offerings to God for his health, and called the place "Jehovah is my standard," meaning "O Jehovah, thou art my high mark. To thee I direct myself in the time of need, as men direct themselves to the standard of the king wherein his camp is in the time of need." Some learned men claim that the name was not called *Nessij*, but *Ness*, without the *ij*, meaning that this altar was to be a standard of a sign to Israel whereby the nations should know what God had done for them in delivering them from Amalek. Therefore it was called *Hanness*, meaning the standard of the sign. Some say it is derived from *Hannoseh*, which is the name given to the angel who is occupied with the affairs of Israel, and this is the interpretation of our most devout and chiefest of poets, our lord Phinehas, in the words to be spoken on the great day of great fasting, and those of his son our lord Abishah. Among the secret properties of this name one is that it contains the exact numerical value of the period our lord Moses lived 120 years (NeSeH=120).

The apostle closed his words with the saying, "The hand is upon the throne of Jehovah. (He has sworn) there will be a war for Jehovah with Amalek from generation to generation." Some explain the last two words forever and ever. This was done so that Joshua might not be carried off with his strength and courage because he destroyed Amalek, but that he might remember that his ability was from God, that he might be humble and attribute nothing to himself. From the word *Kessah* we have now what we call "the verse of the throne," for the word means "throne." And God possesses the best knowledge.

Anyone that desires to learn further, let him read what our learned men have written upon the Sabbath of Amalek. This is all that my sickly intelligence and weak mind has discovered, and we will someday return to God.

XVIII. THE TIME OF JETHRO'S VISIT

A question concerning the story of Jethro: When did he come to his son-in-law? Was it while he was in Rephidim or after? According to the order in the Torah, he arrived at Rephidim before Israel went to Mount Sinai; but we cannot be led with the order, for the words of the Torah may imply the time either before or after. We believe, however, that it is more correct to hold that his visit was on Mount Sinai. Compare Exodus 18:5, "And Jethro, the father-in-law of Moses, came with his sons and his wife to the wilderness where he was encamped, at the mount of God." These words are clear enough, and need no more explanation. According to the commentaries written by that most excellent doctor of blessed memory, Sadakah, his visit to Mount Sinai was in the second year after the erection of the tabernacle. We can prove that from the words given in the fifth book 1:6, "Jehovah our God spoke to us in Horeb, saying, Ye have dwelt long enough in this mountain. Turn and take your journey," etc. Then in the next passage, beginning with verse 9: "And I spake unto you at that time, saying. I am not able to bear you alone myself," etc.

Read the following verses, where he informs us that he established "chiefs of thousands and of hundreds," referring to what Jethro his father-in-law had advised him. Thus we know that it was before their departure from Mount Sinai this new arrangement was done. It was due to Jethro, who gave the advice the very morning of the day when he arrived at where the apostle was, as we read in Exodus 18:13. This passage is the greatest proof to us that Jethro arrived in the beginning of the second year of the departure of the Israelites from Egypt, after the erection of the tabernacle. Therefore no attention should be paid to the suggestion that his visit took place before their entrance into the wilderness of Sinai, for we read in Exodus 18:27, "And Moses sent his father-in-law, who went to his home." Again, we know the departure of Jethro to his land took place during the time when they were about to leave Mount Sinai, as we read in Numbers 10:29, "And Moses said to Jethro, the son of Hobab the Midianite, his father-in-law, 'We are about to leave.'" And he asked him to go with them; but he refused, saying, "No, I cannot go, but I shall go to my land and to my kindred." And this is an additional and plain testimony to our position.

Why Both Hobab and Jethro?

If one asks, "Why was he called here Hobab when his name was Jethro?" We will say that the name Hobab means "loving," and was given to him by the apostle Moses. Compare Deuteronomy 33:3, *Af hobeb ammim*," he loveth (is lover of) the people." He loved piety and offered sacrifices of thanks to God for his great favors to Israel for delivering them from Egypt. Read Exodus 18:10-12, "Blessed be Jehovah, who delivered you from the hand of the Egyptians, and from that of Pharaoh,... and Jethro, Moses' father-in-law, took a burnt offering and sacrifices for God." To those who assert that Jethro knew God only during this visit of his Moses, as verse 11 may indicate, we would say, The conversion of Jethro took place while he was the high priest of Midian, but his people continued in their heathenish way, and he left them, believing in God and in his oneness. That is why the people lost their respect for him, and his daughters were driven away, and not allowed by the shepherds to water their sheep; for it was but right that his sheep should have been given the right of way first and allowed to drink, for Jethro was the high priest. Were it not for his conversion, Moses would not have entered into his family by marrying one of his daughters.

The words of Jethro, *Attah yadaty*, "Now I know," imply only a declaration, but nothing reflecting on his former belief. Having heard of the deeds of God's power and greatness, he renewed his belief in him and his greatness by saying, "God is greater than all the gods."

If one also should say, "Why was not the account of the visit postponed, and recorded at its own place?" We would reply in two ways: first, as it was God's plan to record ordinances and occurrences, some anticipating others, and as the account of Jethro's visit was short, he recorded it here. Second, God may have recorded Jethro's visit in chapter 18 in order that it might be read immediately after the account of the battle with Amalek, that Jethro's superiority and nobility of character might be the more noticed. He was related to Amalek, being the son of Reuel and a descendant of Esau; and Amalek, we know, was the son of Eliphaz, a descendant of Esau. The latter came to do evil to Israel, but the former came to do them good; and that is what prompted Moses to call him Hobab, or "lover," and to be pleased with his counsel, which he obeyed. He therefore asked what may be read in Numbers 10:31-32. A like example and precedent may be found in Genesis, where the account of Judah is given in the story of Joseph, and where it is said that when Judah saw the harlot woman, he went to her, but as to Joseph, when the harlot saw him she sought him, but he ran away from her, and the difference and superiority of the one over the other may be well marked out. Enough. The best knowledge is that of God.

The most learned and wise doctor, Jacob son of Isaak, the physician of Askelon, says, in his book called "The Commentaries of Ordinances," that Jethro made two visits to his son-in-law; first, in company with Moses' wife and two children; and last with the intention of settling down with him and entering into his religion and fulfilling the ordinances, together with all those who moved with him of his children and neighbors, thereby becoming like the Israelites, with the same rights and privileges. It is said that the children of Jethro received a portion of the promised land in preference to the rest of the Gentiles, who were converted to our religion. God alone, however, is infallible.

XIX. THE SONS OF MOSES

To the question, whether the children of Moses, with their mother, returned with Jethro or remained with Moses, I answer, the wife of Moses, or the mother of the children, remained with the apostle without ever being known by him, as we know from Numbers 12:1, "And Miriam and Aaron spake against Moses on account of the beautiful woman whom he had taken." This *ishah*, or "woman," was exactly the same Zeporah, and not, as the Jews pretend, that the apostle Moses took a Cushite woman as wife, *Kusheet*, that is "a black woman." May God fight them for this imputation on the Apostle! The fact is that the apostle Moses did never remarry, not to say that he had married a black woman, a marriage that was quite prohibited, and the Israelites were absolutely forbidden to approach such women. The qualifying word is *Kasheet*, which means "beautiful," and not *Kusheet*, as the Jews had it, meaning "black," thereby reversing the meaning of the passage. (The Samaritans read this word *Kash-sheet*, and derive it from a verb meaning "to grow fat, plump, and beautiful.)

For the apostle, after conversing with God in the burning bush, did never know a woman; and we will prove this in another place, if the Lord wills. As to the children, according to our lord high priest Jacob, in his book entitled "Pleasure Hours," they returned with Jethro; but the apostle, fearing they might go astray after his death, in accordance with what he said in Deuteronomy 31:39, wrote them a copy of the Torah and handed it to them, and sent them in company with their grandfather Jethro. They, however, did not return to their former place, but in company with a party of people, who were to see to the fulfillment of the Torah and its commands, went towards the east, and their descendants are still living; but they had a nomadic life, like the Arabs, dwelling in their hair tents. The writer of the aforesaid book says that their descendants will live unto the end, in their obedience to God. When Moses bade his children good-by, the writer says, he uttered the following words: "Peace be to you, O Gershom and Eliezer!" This was a covenant of peace, a guarantee from all dangers, and it would not be possible that their race be cut off to the end of the world. Only Jehovah had concealed them and set them afar, that none may know their whereabouts until he permits it. And God knows best!

XX. THE HEIR OF AN ADULTERESS

Question: Should a man take to himself a woman as his wife whom he discovers afterwards to have violated her purity, and who is adjudged to be killed; if she is killed, who will be her heir?

Her heir will be the high priest who adjudges her to death. None else, whether he be a relative or neighbor, or even her husband, can inherit the least thing from her. This can be inferred from Numbers 5:5-8, "When a man or woman commit any sin... if the person have no kinsman to whom restitution may be made for the guilt, such restitution that is made unto Jehovah for guilt must be the priest's." The writer of this answer compares it with the case of the inheritance of the daughters of Zelophehad, who would not have inherited their father, unless it were for the fact that he did rebel against God, for they said: "He was not among them that gathered themselves against Jehovah in the company of Korah: but he died in his own sin" (Numbers 27:3). His sin resulted from his work on the Sabbath: on that day he was discovered felling wood, which was not rebellion, and therefore his daughters deserved to inherit him. The unbeliever or rebellious, according to our learned men, can neither inherit nor be inherited. It is said that in such a case as we have already mentioned, the money advanced, or whatever was promised to the woman by the husband before the marriage to be paid by him after the marriage, even if it were advanced to her previous to the discovery of her guilt, the same forms a part of her inheritance, and he can lay no claim to it. And God knows the unknown.

XXI. THE FACE OF LABAN

Why is it that in Genesis 31:2, "And Jacob saw the face of Laban, and, behold, they were not *Eynam* as before," the plural form is used? The reading *Eynam* refers surely as well to the children of Laban. For the first verse reads, "And he heard the words of Laban's sons, saying, Jacob hath taken away all that was our father's." Thus *Eynam* refers to them as well as to their father. Our lord Jacob discovered the inner change of Laban from that of his face; for nothing he concealed within himself but leaked through the features of his face and the utterances of his tongue. The countenance of man is the mirror of his soul. Some say that the sharp sight of the believer unveils the inner soul. But God knows best.

XXII. CONCERNING OATHS

How can you harmonize the command of the decalogue, "Do not pronounce the name of Jehovah thy God in vain," and the one, "Do not swear falsely in my name," with "His words he shall not unbind or break"? Answer: The command given in Deuteronomy 5:11, meaning, "Thou shalt not raise" etc., really does not mean to prohibit something the carrying of which is sinful, nor the raising or lifting of an object from one place to another; but the command means simply, "Do not pronounce" the name of the Most High in false utterances, just as we have the same words *Lo tish-sha* in the prohibitive command *Lo tish-sha shoma* show, meaning, "Do not pronounce or raise a false report" avoid spreading reports of the veracity of which you are not sure. Our learned men have divided oaths under three heads.

First, the prohibited oath of falsehood, as meaning "Thou shalt not bear false witness against thy neighbor," and "Thou shalt not bear vain or untruthful witness."

Second, the prohibited oath for selling or buying commodities either without weight or measure, but by mere guesswork.

Third, the prohibited oaths which are made for no purpose whatever, and nothing is affirmed or denied thereby. From the command "Thou shalt not swear falsely in My name," we may infer that an oath may be either obligatory, or lawful, or vicious. The first is the right of the one accused of crime but without evidence. The oath is to be made in the court before the judge, for Jehovah said, "In My name thou shalt swear"; also, "The oath of Jehovah shall be between them." The lawful oath is that which binds a man to performance if the act be lawful; as, refraining from eating, drinking, fasting, and wearing costly apparels, etc. The oath in such cases is binding, and must be carried out. The vicious oath is that which is made falsely, coupling the name of the Most High God with things unlikely or false, and thereby dishonoring him. Compare "Ye shall not swear falsely in My name, and thus profane the name of thy God. I am Jehovah."

The punishment of such a transgression must be meted out with death. The transgressor profanes the name God by such an oath, made in any other tongue. As to Leviticus 5:2, it means that the swearer rashly must be bound to his oath, if sin is not to be committed; but if his oath is due to causes which render him unconscious of his oath, such as drinking, be is not responsible; if conscious, he is quite responsible and must carry out his obligation. Then God said, "He shall not break his word; he shall do according to all that which proceeded out of his mouth."

Our learned men have written with great zeal concerning the import of "Thou shalt not pronounce the name of Jehovah thy God falsely." Of the many allusions this passage contains, one is to the hypocrite, who shows piety to the world, but who is secretly attached to his sins and to a life of immorality, a slave to his passions, and therefore his connection with God is groundless, and the pronunciation of God's name is in vain, and untrue to his conviction. Therefore God said: "For Jehovah will not hold him guiltless, who pronounces his name falsely." Clear! The man whose conduct is so characterized is more afraid of the creature than of the Creator, and cannot be guiltless before God, for his false oath. Every word of God as given in the revealed Torah through our lord Moses (upon whom be peace) possesses several allusions which are to be applied in their proper places. This is enough for the man who lays aside his prejudice, and is willing to receive guidance and act piously. In all such things let God be the final judge, and let the sentence he utters be carried out. This is all which a tired mind and sickly intelligence could discover. But the Most High knows best what is ideally right.

XXIII. THE INHERITANCE OF A WOMAN WHO MARRIES OUTSIDE THE TRIBE

If a man should die leaving behind him wealth, such as land, etc., but no male heir who may legally inherit him; if he should be survived by daughters, married in families other than his and outside of the tribe, what should be done with the wealth of the defunct? Have the daughters any rightful claim on them or not? What would follow? The answer (praise be to God only) is as follows. The daughters who are the only offspring of their parents should marry their cousins of their tribe, if they desire valid claim to their shares, in order that the inheritance may continue to be theirs. Remember that the daughters of Zelophehad, when their request was granted, were conditioned to marry in the tribe of their father; for the inheritance should never pass from one tribe to another. Our predecessors (may God be pleased with them) said, and their saying must be obeyed, that even if the daughter who has inherited from her father should desire to marry a man outside of her tribe she would be disinherited, and others worthier than she, who belong to the tribe, would receive the inheritance. This statement is absolute, and liable to no modification. The land of the defunct should not be transferred to his daughters who are his only heirs, but who have married into another tribe. The inheritance of their father must remain intact: another tribe is not to enjoy its use. It must be preserved and carefully guarded until God's purpose is made manifest relative to the daughters of the defunct. Should their husbands die, they are entitled to the inheritance; should they die, the inheritance becomes the property of the House of God, if there is none that may have a legal claim to it. Compare Numbers 5:8, "And if there is no kinsman to the man that restitution may be made to him for the guilt, the restitution that is made for the guilt unto Jehovah shall belong to the priest." The restitution to the priest is made as if to the House of God. This is according to our understanding of the law and to the exact interpretation of our learned men. But the Most High God knows best the exact truth. Verily he knows the unknown.

XXIV. THE USE OF RENNET

Some of my people asked me concerning the use made by our predecessors of the rennet of the suckling kid, in order to make cheese, by placing it in milk, and the continuance of this custom until the attention of the humble writer was called to it, resulting in its abolition; and since then we have not discovered any using it. As to the use of the rennet by our people, I may say it is surely a great vice which our people introduced inadvertently. They had either taken it from the Jews, or had been deceived into adopting it by some indifferent believers in the days of Benutan. Nobody seemed to have spoken against the practice, as it is evident many generations had come and passed without the least attention having been called to it.

If one should ask, "How could this have taken place during all this time and period, the length of which is unknown, and none of the former learned and able men had ever attempted to oppose and prohibit the practice?" For an answer, I can only say that God, in his divine foreknowledge, knew that doubtless some faults would be unknowingly committed by his hosts, and their eyes could not discover them, and therefore, he said in Leviticus 4:13, "And if the whole congregation of Israel shall err, and a certain thing be hid from the eyes of the assembly." Otherwise no need of this passage would have been found. No guilt is therefore to be laid on us, or on those who preceded us, for this past practice; for it was due to a general inadvertence. Behold how careful we are in our use of meat in connection with milk or milk in connection with meat. Should a vessel have the least trace of flesh or milk; should it not even be very clean, and then any of the two substances, flesh or milk, be placed in it, it becomes, according to us, *Tamay*, that is, "defiled." Even if the salt that touched the meat be used with milk, the same state of pollution would follow, and we could not use the milk.

The rennet is, in reality, one of the portions of the sheep or kid that belong to the priest, and should be immediately delivered to him, and no delay made: for it is *Kadosh*, "holy." Since it contains milk, and the butcher removes it and cuts it while both his knife and hands are stained with flesh and blood, it becomes binding to us to have nothing to do with its use as food, if we are to be faithful to our tradition and practices. I, therefore, in order to keep my religious duties, have put its use under the ban. Its eating is neither necessary nor binding, and we have neither command nor law to that effect; but we use it as we use butter and fat and the like. It is unlike the unleavened bread and the sacrifices of the Passover which must be eaten. We must not defile our souls by a doubtful thing which we can easily do. God said, "Do not defile your souls," and "Ye shall be holy to God" etc. This is sufficient. To obey is safest, and God knows best.

XXV. THE ABRIDGMENT BY LAYMEN OF THE AUTHORITY OF THE PRIESTHOOD

A few men of the laity protested that they should be "associates" of the Scribes in giving judgments and supervising the estates of the priesthood. Can there be any attention paid to them and have they any right to their claim? If what they claim is vain, please give them a confuting reply, and convict them strongly of their vicious pretensions; and may the kind giver reward you!

The answer: The noble Torah gives the children of Levi complete authority over all the estates or offerings of the temple. None else can have any hand in these matters. Thus said God in Numbers 18:1, "And Jehovah said to Aaron, 'Thou and thy sons and thy fathers' house with thee shall bear the iniquity of the sanctuary. And thou and thy sons with thee shall bear the iniquity of your priesthood. And thy brethren also, the line of Levi, the tribe of thy father, draw them near with thee, that they will be responsible as he was.'" God foreknew that the descendants of Aaron are the children of Levi. Again, we are plainly told that in whatever matter not indicated by the law, the decision of the priests, the sons of Levi, should prevail, and could not be modified unless by some legal reasons. Read Deuteronomy 18:8, "If there be concealed from thee a matter in judging, as between blood and blood, between plea and plea, or stroke and stroke, matters of controversy... arise, and go up to the place, which Jehovah thy God has chosen, to the Levite priests." Their decision is binding, as we read in verse 10, "according to the decision they shall tell thee thou shalt do; thou shalt not turn aside from the sentence they shall show thee, neither to the right nor to the left." The same is affirmed in those things set apart for God: "Then the priest shall value it, whether it be good or bad; as the priest shall value it, so it shall stand" (Leviticus 27:14).

In addition, I must say that, from Scriptural inferences, the high priest of the people must have his due honor. None should injure his name or measure up himself beyond him, as one may do with others. His people should pay him their respects and esteem, and should not look at him as any of their ordinary fellow citizens. Distinction and preference should be given all his people, for it is apparent to all intelligent people that not every man of any grade could be made into a high priest, lest his practices humiliate him and keep him aloof, lest God be displeased and his worship be vain; this especially given with reference to the Levites, who are, as the righteous Lord has said, the chosen persons for priesthood, prayer, blessing, and divine judgments. Compare

Deuteronomy 18:5, "For Jehovah thy God has chosen him out of all thy tribes, that he may stand to serve in the name of Jehovah, he and his sons all the days." This means that they were chosen from ancient days to be honored and respected.

I have found, also, that the Levite must not be discarded and others followed: "Beware of discarding the Levite the length of thy days on earth," (Deuteronomy 12:19). It is in connection with the tribe of Levi that the apostle Moses made the prayer found in Deuteronomy 33:11, that its prayers may be heard, and blessings may be bestowed;" that its enemies may be crushed, as "O Jehovah, bless his strength, and be pleased with the works of his hands." A warning is given that the Levite may not be opposed, as we read in the same verse: "But break through the loins of those that rebel against him and hate him." The learned Hasam Assoory of Tyrus explains these words as follows: He who harbors any evil thing or hatred against this tribe, Jehovah will smite him with great calamities, and his plans will fail; for the prayers or curses of the Levites shoot through faster than the very arrows. As to the words "Break through the loins of his opposers and haters," they mean that he who would plan to do such things is only a darer, who is unaware of his conditions, and is like the man who drinks poison to try it. To impress the people with dire consequences of such an attempt, he says, "Who could oppose him?" Therefore, I believe that it is not lawful to depart at any time from their given decisions and pleasures, nor is it lawful to call a halt to them through reasons of expediency, on merely mental grounds for they have been long before empowered by the declarations of the Torah, and it is not to be imagined that the decisions of others are applicable to them unless there is against them a legal plea. And God knows best.

Now I ask you readers of this my epistle to explain to me the exact meaning of the words of Jehovah in Deuteronomy 19:14, "Thou shalt not remove the landmarks of thy neighbors which the ancients have set up." What meaning do you put on the word *Reeshoneem*, "first ones," "ancient ones"? God has affirmed this command with strong terms, for he said, "Cursed be the man who changes the landmarks of his neighbor."

Pray, inform me, also, concerning the meaning of the words, "Thou shalt love thy neighbor as thyself. I am God." How contrary to this command do we act! How we do hate each other, and how we do backbite each other! To these things is due our downfall and utter relapse. So much is sufficient.

And, as for the rest, though it is unknown to me, and I understand not even the boundaries of that which I know not, it is definite in the mind of God, and he knows all. Amen.

WRITTEN ON THE 29th DAY OF SHEWAL, CORRESPONDING TO THE 21st OF NOVEMBER OF THE ARABIC YEAR 1325 (1907 A.D.), BY ITS HUMBLE AUTHOR JACOB, THE PRIEST OF THE SAMARITAN PEOPLE IN NABLOUS.

BIBLIOTHECA SACRA

A Religious and Sociological Quarterly

Editor

G. Frederick Wright

Single Number, 75 cents
Yearly Subscription, $3.00

Oberlin, Ohio. USA
BIBLIOTHECA SACRA COMPANY

European Agents: Charles Higham & Son
27a Farringdon St., London, E.C.

Made in the USA
Lexington, KY
28 December 2018